THE
LONGEST CAST

This book is dedicated, with love, to my mother, Margaretta Taylor

THE LONGEST CAST

THE FLY-FISHING JOURNEY OF A LIFETIME

PHOTOGRAPHY BY PETER AND BEVERLY PICKFORD
FOREWORD BY LEFTY KREH

ALEXANDER TAYLOR

NEW HOLLAND

CHAPTER NINE
ALASKA
CHAPTER SEVEN
SCOTLAND
CHAPTER SIX
IRELAND
CHAPTER EIGHT
BAHAMAS
CHAPTER ONE
BOTSWANA
CHAPTER TWO
SOUTH AFRICA
CHAPTER THREE
ARGENTINA

CHAPTER FIVE
BHUTAN

CHAPTER FOUR
NEW ZEALAND

CONTENTS

FOREWORD

If you have ever longed to travel to remote parts of the world to fly fish, this book will help you fulfill that quest. It is a visual feast of the places most fly fishermen dream of. Peter and Beverly Pickford have captured the magic of fly-fishing on film, and the photography is outstanding! Some of the photos will explain to the viewer what a visiting angler could never put into words. Alex's essays and chapters are gripping, and tie the whole thing together.

Fly-fishing is much more than catching fish – and so is this book. I have been blessed during my fly-fishing life to visit many remote and distant places. So many times the memories of those trips don't involve the fish caught.

Once, in western New Guinea on the Bensbach River, we met a native paddling a dugout filled with watermelons. This area is so remote that the natives there still live much as they did a thousand years ago. There are no roads, no electricity, no radio or television. The friendly Aborigine offered us several watermelons, but only if we brought back the seeds – they were needed for replanting in the absence of any stores. On that same trip, while we were having lunch in the shade on one bank, we watched two Aborigines use their bows and arrows to down a kangaroo.

On my first fishing trip to the remote Kimberleys of Northern Australia's Outback, I caught 18 species of fish that I had never previously seen. Although we had great fun and excitement catching those fish, the elements that made the trip one of my most memorable were the 10,000-year-old cave paintings, the 18-foot crocodile that hung out in a billabong near our tent camp, and the flock of huge fruit bats that clouded the evening sky as they left a nearby roost.

I have visited Alaska many times, and on some trips the number of fish caught has been almost incalculable. But one of the most remarkable trips was when a falling 18-foot tide stranded our floatplane high on a gravel bank. Waiting for the rising water, we had to sleep for several hours on the beach. It was chilly, and we had no warm clothing. The old timer with us instructed each of us to dig a shallow pit in the shoreline gravel about six feet in length. Using driftwood from the beach, we built a fire in each pit, and when it had been reduced to glowing embers he had us pile the gravel on top. Lying down on the gravel, we placed our rain gear over us and slept as snug as if we were on a warm waterbed.

Fishing around the world makes you realize that it is the culture and the history that surround you that make a trip so enjoyable. The artistic skills of Peter, Beverly, and Alex have captured the essence of what it is like to travel to remote places, a feat that is nearly impossible for the rest of us. The Pickfords' unbelievable early-morning and late-evening photos of the native birds, the pictures of animals caught in unusual poses, incredible shots of fly-fishing and the fish caught, as well as photos of the indigenous people, make this a very special volume. Alex has done the unthinkable in compiling all of this material into one beautiful book. If you yearn to discover the world of fly-fishing, *The Longest Cast* will fill you with joy.

Lefty Kreh

FOREWORD

If you have ever longed to travel to remote parts of the world to fly fish, this book will help you fulfill that quest. It is a visual feast of the places most fly fishermen dream of. Peter and Beverly Pickford have captured the magic of fly-fishing on film, and the photography is outstanding! Some of the photos will explain to the viewer what a visiting angler could never put into words. Alex's essays and chapters are gripping, and tie the whole thing together.

Fly-fishing is much more than catching fish – and so is this book. I have been blessed during my fly-fishing life to visit many remote and distant places. So many times the memories of those trips don't involve the fish caught.

Once, in western New Guinea on the Bensbach River, we met a native paddling a dugout filled with watermelons. This area is so remote that the natives there still live much as they did a thousand years ago. There are no roads, no electricity, no radio or television. The friendly Aborigine offered us several watermelons, but only if we brought back the seeds – they were needed for replanting in the absence of any stores. On that same trip, while we were having lunch in the shade on one bank, we watched two Aborigines use their bows and arrows to down a kangaroo.

On my first fishing trip to the remote Kimberleys of Northern Australia's Outback, I caught 18 species of fish that I had never previously seen. Although we had great fun and excitement catching those fish, the elements that made the trip one of my most memorable were the 10,000-year-old cave paintings, the 18-foot crocodile that hung out in a billabong near our tent camp, and the flock of huge fruit bats that clouded the evening sky as they left a nearby roost.

I have visited Alaska many times, and on some trips the number of fish caught has been almost incalculable. But one of the most remarkable trips was when a falling 18-foot tide stranded our floatplane high on a gravel bank. Waiting for the rising water, we had to sleep for several hours on the beach. It was chilly, and we had no warm clothing. The old timer with us instructed each of us to dig a shallow pit in the shoreline gravel about six feet in length. Using driftwood from the beach, we built a fire in each pit, and when it had been reduced to glowing embers he had us pile the gravel on top. Lying down on the gravel, we placed our rain gear over us and slept as snug as if we were on a warm waterbed.

Fishing around the world makes you realize that it is the culture and the history that surround you that make a trip so enjoyable. The artistic skills of Peter, Beverly, and Alex have captured the essence of what it is like to travel to remote places, a feat that is nearly impossible for the rest of us. The Pickfords' unbelievable early-morning and late-evening photos of the native birds, the pictures of animals caught in unusual poses, incredible shots of fly-fishing and the fish caught, as well as photos of the indigenous people, make this a very special volume. Alex has done the unthinkable in compiling all of this material into one beautiful book. If you yearn to discover the world of fly-fishing, *The Longest Cast* will fill you with joy.

Lefty Kreh

THE FLY-FISHING
JOURNEY OF A LIFETIME
INTRODUCTION

I believe that fly-fishing is the most spiritually satisfying sport in existence. Ever since I picked up my first Orvis fly rod, at the age of 10 or 11, I have been fascinated with all facets of fly-fishing – the rods, fly lines, trout habits, and, most importantly, the waters. The mystery of fishing and the many factors that come together in such a tricky, yet peaceful, activity as I strive to capture a creature that inhabits a totally different world, keep me always dreaming of rivers and pure mountain air.

There are places I can go, and things I can see, that Nature only allows me because of my fly rod. Far from the hustle and confusion of my other life, and far into the wilderness, there is another world – a world of serenity, a place where a noise that would not even be heard in a house full of family and friends can electrify you. A leaping fish, a startled deer, even an eagle diving to feed – these are sights and memories that only happen in places set aside by Nature as temples of purity, places so perfect that you feel you are standing in an invisible light so powerful you can almost feel it warming your soul. I went around the world with Peter and Beverly

Pickford, two of the finest people and photographers you will find anywhere on Earth. Contained in the pages of this book are images and thoughts that would never normally make it out of their private watery sanctuaries. We combined our skills of observation – mine in words, theirs in images – to capture the essence of what fly-fishing is, or can be, today.

I often say that fly-fishing has grown to become like a large and beautiful tree, laden with character and age. Over the centuries since it first took root, its branches have spread throughout the world into many different cultures. Today, you can go almost anywhere on Earth and not be far from someone with a fly rod. While I once thought this was a bad thing that interfered with my own solitude on the water, I am now happy to see another fly-fisherman on a lonely stretch of river. The culture that we, as fly-fishermen, have created is a very pleasing and positive response to Nature.

Our ignorance of the unknown leads us to make mistakes, and Nature has suffered in many ways because of that. But fly-fishermen, on the whole, are people who

LEFT: *Aleutian Range, Iliamna, Alaska.*

value the essence of the places they visit. The fish we catch are smart, and more in tune with their surroundings than we are. Of course, throwing them a hook with a worm on it would often catch a fish more quickly, but the time and care it takes to entice a fish to take a fly generates respect for the impenetrable world of nature. An old fly-fishing saying goes something like, "It doesn't matter whether you catch a fish or not." I believe that the more fly-fishermen come to care for and respect our world, the better. It may sound arrogant, but I hope that

here in this book you will see what I mean – there are few finer cultures on Earth than that of fly-fishing.

It would be impossible to capture all the fly-fishing spots in the world, but we went to many of the great ones, and to some others you may not have known about. To my knowledge, this has never been done before. There are other books about worldwide fly-fishing. In fact, there is fly-fishing literature dating back to medieval times but, until now, no one has ever made one continuous trip around the world, stopping along the

BELOW: *Bonefishing from a skiff, Moxey Town, Andros Island, Bahamas.*

ABOVE: *Beside the camp fire, Okavango, Botswana.*

way to fish the greatest of places, and produced a book solely to capture the beauty of that fishing journey.

Moreover, although many photographic books on fishing visit beautiful places and beautiful waters, the photographers have usually felt the need to alter the purity of the image with filters or other tricks. Quite often, a photographer will try to create the effect of a sunset when in fact it is midday. Peter and Beverly do not believe in these techniques. They are intent on capturing nature exactly as nature is. The only filter they possess is a polarizing filter, to reduce glare on the water. All the images you see in this book were captured through pure patience and persistence. Personally, I think it is the best photography ever done on the sport. Peter and Beverly are as difficult to track down as an Atlantic salmon. They dissolve themselves into Nature, and no doubt they will

be thousands of miles from sight and sound when this book comes out, but I would still like to thank them for their friendship and for all they put into this book. If ever I met two people who love the great outdoors as much as I do, it is they.

As for my part, I have tried to put into words what I can normally only ever feel when fishing. This was a difficult process that took time to evolve. Botswana, being the first stop on the trip, contains an essay about the jitters and fun of catching a tiger fish. But, it was not until I reached Argentina, the third stop, that I finally began to reach a little farther inside myself to discover what swirls around my mind when I'm wading out into a river. From there on, you will find an essay at the start of each chapter that attempts to capture the complexities of what a fly-fishermen thinks about in many of the different situations he finds himself in around the world. (When I say he, it is only out of habit. Women are quite often the most graceful and talented anglers to be found.)

From Bhutan to Alaska, and everywhere in between, I give you what I wrote in my journal from the banks of the rivers we were fishing. Each essay was written streamside. The thoughts sometimes sway from reality to abstraction. My mind wanders from a dry fly or a back eddy to any one of the vast waves of thoughts or feelings that overcome me when I fish. Sometimes I will think about someone I once loved, or someone I still do; I might think about my late father or the tranquility of being alone. Yet, wherever we were, I wrote what I felt.

Many people have asked me what made me want to put this book together. I usually spout out something about how I love to travel and fish, and how I wanted to do it all while I was still young. But, the real reason is that it just had to be done. The places we went, and the things we saw, are some of the most beautiful anywhere on Earth. Lest something should happen to them, they have to be recorded and recognized in their purity.

Before the Industrial Revolution, fishermen caught salmon in Beaufort, South Carolina. Since then, temperatures have risen and, of course, the salmon are no longer there or most other places they were once found. Rivers all around the world are slowly becoming unsuitable habitats for fish and other wildlife. By the end of this century, it is estimated that average temperatures will rise by about 10 degrees Fahrenheit. Trout will be forced to move ever further up the mountains to escape.

If we are not careful, one day some of the places we see in this book will no longer exist as they are today.

BELOW: *Fly-fishermen on horseback, Mount Anderson Ranch, Lydenburg, South Africa.*

ABOVE: *On the crystal-clear waters of the Rio Grande, Patagonia, Argentina.*

But the spirit behind this book may, with a little luck, put that day off for a while. With every rise to a fly, someone is becoming more and more intoxicated by the beauty of this sport and its world. Swirling behind every rock, and stirring at the bottom of every pool, are answers to the questions we ask ourselves in our dreams. One day, enough people may come to love this facet of Nature, and realize that making ourselves a part of the wild from time to time may just ensure that our descendants derive as much pleasure from all that God has given us as we have.

Every time I see a young child voluntarily release a fish, it makes me smile. It makes me think that perhaps the ignorant spoiling of the wild may one day be tempered by respect, moderation, and love for Mother Nature, and that my grandchildren will one day be able to enjoy releasing a trout into the Gunnison or the Copper River. And, maybe, I will be able to return to Scotland when I am old to catch another salmon before they are all gone.

Alex Taylor

TIGERS IN THE DARK
BOTSWANA

NXAMASERI CAMP, NXAMASERI, BOTSWANA

We awoke at five o'clock this morning at the beautiful Nxamaseri Camp, bleary-eyed, yet filled with the excitement and expectations of all that one might expect from the Okavango Delta. During the night, I had dreamt exotic dreams of jungle, wild animals, sunlight and darkness, and rain. As we slept, we could hear night owls sweeping the sky for food. Monkeys were busy leaping from tree to tree. And then, as always, Africa makes a couple of sounds you just cannot quite put your finger on — what was that loud thud just outside your tent?

We were in Botswana, where, preying in the flooding waters outside, somewhere in the darkness, was one of the world's least known sport fish — the ferocious tiger fish. Waiting for us like trained prizefighters, the tigers swilled their bodies violently through the dark as we obsessively planned our hunt. Like knights preparing to joust, we were all bonded together by a great camaraderie as we carefully prepared our gear, single-mindedly focused on the shared goal of finding the truth within the river.

LEFT: *Fishing at sunset on the Okavango River, Okavango.*

I spent the first 20 minutes of my day sitting before a single silver hook in my vice. I pulled feathers from the back of a chicken, cut the hair from the quarters of a deer, and I missed breakfast with the others in order to design what would be the perfect fly for the day. I tied these materials to the hook with seven strands of peacock herl on the top to create what is known as a Lefty's Deceiver. Tying a set of weighted lead eyes on to the front, I completed what I hoped would be the perfect Okavango fly, which I named the Taylor's Tiger Fisher.

No sooner had I left my tent than we were skating along the smooth water out to the main river – basking in the all-encompassing glow of an African sunrise. We were in the lodge's custom-built, flat-bottom boat, muscling our way through the morning air to intercept the beast as it fed. Unaware of our intentions, this

"… we were all bonded together by a great camaraderie as we carefully prepared our gear, single-mindedly focused on the shared goal of finding the truth within the river."

RIGHT: *This tiger fish, caught in the Okavango river, shows how acrobatic they can be. They take to the fly hard, and wrestle with it both above and below the surface. Because their mouths are so bony and filled with teeth, they can often spit the fly out on a jump like this. Setting the hook well is an important component of tiger fishing.*

fierce African fish waited ahead, arrogantly and ruthlessly devouring baitfish with the strength and energy that so typifies African wildlife.

Double-hauling my first cast at the junction of two tributaries, I set the fly down into the water with a delicate red splash, and a ring that silently circled away. Strip, strip, strip – pause. Strip, strip, strip – pause. My fly was fortunate enough to make it back to the boat unharmed, but, showing no respect for the beautiful fly that I had so painstakingly constructed only an hour before, I thrust it back through the air with every intention of seeing it destroyed and consumed by the dangerous jaws of my prey.

Several minutes passed as my fly repeatedly returned to the boat, no doubt with a growing smile of relief. Riding up and down on the swirls and eddies that continuously revolved beneath the surface, this fly began to seem as though it just might make it back, unharmed, to its luxurious bed in my leather fly case. Then, whoosh! A sudden rush of water startled the calm surface. Three feet of free line instantly seared through my hand. I had been foolishly wrapping the line through my fingers as I stripped, but as soon as I was able to release it, the line paid out through my burning fingers. Immediately alert, I saw the rod bent over the side of the boat, honorably doing its duty. The line fizzled through the water as the fish

darted upstream. Then panicking, wondering why his little breakfast had turned into such a nightmare, the tiger broke through the surface, exposing his silver shine and the fiery red tail that these fish so elegantly carry behind them. Plush! He landed back in the water, realizing that something was certainly wrong.

The fight was quickly over, and I proudly enjoyed the fisherman's favorite feeling of holding his first catch of the morning. With a subdued smile, and an invigorated spirit, I gently released the monster to fight another day. As he rushed back to the safety of the deep water, I bade goodbye to this fabulous fish. Now more wary and wise, he was joining the ranks of the experienced who feed with more caution and greater confidence from darker depths, those who may not be seen again until they are worthy of being called a trophy, and are the fitting subject of a hopeful angler's warm dreams.

A BRIEF HISTORY

For millennia, the voracious tiger fish (*Hydrocynus vittatus*) has terrorized the dark waters of central and southern Africa. However, the process of initiating them into the world of international fly-fishing has been a very recent development. In fact, the tiger fish in Africa and the taimen in Mongolia are probably the world's two newest fly-fishing challenges.

The fish is distributed throughout Africa – they can be found in the Nile, the Congo River, the Lualaba, Lake Tanganyika, and many other large lake and river systems. The most popular fishing locations are the Zambezi River – which runs through Zambia, Zimbabwe, and Mozambique – and the Okavango Delta that floods the plains of Botswana.

European penetration into central Africa did not occur in earnest until the Renaissance, when sea-faring communities began to explore the world around them. In the early 16th century, the Portuguese were the first outsiders to explore central Africa, but in the decades and centuries thereafter, Europeans began to arrive in droves to exploit the cheap ivory and rubber resources. This eventually culminated, at the end of the 19th century, in King Leopold II's shameful ravaging of the African populations in the Congo River basin area of central Africa. No doubt, these intrepid explorers experienced the excitement of catching the mighty tiger fish, since the tiger will feed on almost anything that moves and is small enough for its mouth.

In the meantime, in 1856, the Royal Geographic Society sponsored a trip, led by Richard Burton, to discover the source of the Nile. These explorers collected numerous samples of organisms, flora and fauna, and large animals and fish previously unknown to science. One of these fish was the tiger fish. Once these samples had been taken back to England and studied, they were admitted into the world of science. In 1861, French ichthyologist François Laporte, Count Castelnau, formally declared the tiger fish a unique fish species, naming it *Hydrocynus vittatus*.

Artificial flies were known in Africa then, as the colonialists had introduced trout throughout southern and eastern Africa. However, there are no records of anyone fly-fishing for tigers at that time. For more than another century, this explosive fish lived in obscurity, rendering itself only as a food source for the people who lived along the rivers of central and southern Africa. Not until the 1940s and '50s did trout fishermen, trying their luck with salmon fly rods and tackle brought from England, land the first tigers to be taken on a fly. Reports at the time record that the tigers were caught on artificial flies, but there is no indication of the success, or lack thereof, of these early efforts.

One of the great pioneers of the sport is Phillip deMoor, an African author and fishing expert. Although the history of tiger fishing is not well documented, many people point to Phillip as the first man to set out specifically to pursue the tiger fish – and succeed. He did this in 1965, after the Kariba Dam was constructed in Zimbabwe (then Rhodesia). During the months of October and November, Phillip remembers thousands of tiger fish "spreading out behind the dam wall to

BELOW, *Seeing a tail this size, it isn't hard to imagine the speed and strength with which a tiger fish can fight. This is not to mention the ferocious teeth with which they mangle their prey. You need a long, wire-mesh net to land a tiger fish. It must be wire because the fish destroy any normal net with their teeth. It must be long, because if a crocodile catches you leaning out of the boat for a tiger fish, you might be the catch of the day!*

ascend the Zambezi River where it entered the lake to seek breeding sites in the River and in its tributaries." In documenting this trip, and bringing it to the attention of the fishing fraternity, deMoor formally began the sport of taking tiger fish on a fly. After this landmark trip, however, history conspired to curtail his fly-fishing excursions to the Zambezi until the 1980s.

It was in that decade that the fish in the Okavango were first introduced to an artificial fly. The first record I have been able to come across of anyone taking an Okavango Delta tiger on a fly is in 1986, when the Orvis Fly-fishing Company came to the Okavango Delta under the leadership of the legendary Lee Perkins. They stayed at Nxamaseri and fished for tigers with local guru P.J. Bestelink. With this type of publicity, the sport soon gained some international popularity.

In 1988, Belgian fly-fishing expert Jean van Loock contacted Phillip deMoor and expressed interest in setting the first world records for fly-fishing for tigers. At that time, no formal records were held in any fly-fishing weight, as very few people had entered the arena. Over the next couple of years, these two men not only set every world record in the sport, but also discovered all of the pertinent information regarding the tiger fish's behavior and lifestyle.

Thanks to the pioneering efforts of Phillip deMoor and Jean van Loock, the mystery of the dark waters of Africa was partly revealed, and fly-fishing for tigers is now a common event, even though it is somewhat off the beaten track.

Almost all the fish caught on light fly tackle are males, as these fish tend to congregate in schools along the edges of currents and along the banks. They are frequently found feeding at or near the surface. The larger fish are females, who tend to hug the bottom where the current is less strong. Getting down to them requires a fast sinking fly-line, and a good deal of luck. Many of the large African rivers are very strong and very deep.

In the late 1980s, P.J. Bestelink opened Nxamaseri Camp, which became the first fly-fishing outpost in the Okavango Delta. We were fortunate enough to fish with P.J. himself and his friend and expert fly-fishing partner, Guy, at Nxamaseri. It was an unforgettable experience. P.J. has since become a part of the Botswana landscape. He now runs a horseback safari operation in the bush, and Nxamaseri has been taken over by former partners.

They still fish for tigers with a fly, and the sport is as great as it has ever been. If you are fortunate enough to make it to southern Africa, you may catch a glimpse of a lone fly-fisherman drifting down the Okavango or Zambezi. If it is on the Okavango, and the person is drifting in a makuro, a dug out tree used as a canoe, it may be P.J. On the Zambezi, you might find Phillip, but thanks to these early pioneers, people from all around the world have visited this spot, which has become one of the newest and youngest shoots of the international fly-fishing tree.

THE BOTSWANA EXPERIENCE

Although fishing for tiger fish on the Okavango Delta involves no unusual physical activities, the whole experience is quite different from almost any other fishing trip. For one thing, you have to be careful of the water – you can't just wade right out there! Furthermore, while most destinations reveal amazing sights to you, Africa may stun and even frighten you with its absolutely raw beauty.

The Okavango Delta is an endless maze of canals and stretches, all moving in one direction from northern Botswana to the south. How the guides successfully navigate these passageways amazes me. Each new turn reveals a different view of Botswana; each stretch and pool has a different character.

Some places will reveal hippos (the most dangerous of all your fishing companions), some stretches have crocodiles sleeping on the bank. Eagles swoop down and pick fish out of the water, and sometimes you see natives passing along in their makuro. Stops for lunch breaks on small islands can quickly turn into bird and wildlife safaris.

The fishing you will be doing here is from boats – big strong boats. If you go into the water, you are immediately at the mercy of the crocodiles and the hippos; I stayed in the boat except for a few very quick swims on very hot days.

The boats will drift you along very prolific runs of the river. Almost everywhere we fished produced good numbers of tigers. You'll want to cast into the bank as close as possible and strip the fly back to the boat at various depths, depending on the temperature of the water. My personal favorite was in the morning, when we used poppers on the surface of the calm water.

Tiger fish, three-spot bream, and barbel are the only fish you'll catch. All are edible, but the lodge mainly exercises a catch-and-release policy. The tigers have sharp teeth, which makes every catch a delicate exercise, almost like catching a piranha. The days are idyllic as you drift along endless miles of water lined on each bank with papyrus trees. Standing on the bow of the boat, you'll cover any nook or cranny that looks good, and a great many of them are just that. This is certain to be the experience of a lifetime.

OPPOSITE: *A fish eagle prepares to take a tiger fish right out of Guy's hand. It's a more delicate trick than it looks. These eagles have razor-like talons, and can take your fingers off in an instant. At the end of each day, Guy would stop at the entrance to this pond and make an eagle call. Once it had swooped into a nearby tree, Guy would pass by holding the fish aloft. The eagle would then fall in behind, and snatch it. It took Guy years of leaving a fish behind in the water to train the bird to do this. Now they trust each other, and the bird won't take a fish from anyone else.*

OPPOSITE: *As dusk approaches, the fishing tends to pick up. And so does the insect life. The cool shirt that keeps the sun off during the day offers some protection, but insect repellent is an absolute must in the evenings.*

TACKLE AND GEAR

ROD AND REEL

The fish are not too large, but you'll need to get long casts in order to cover a lot of water. I fished with my 9-weight almost every day. There will be times when you're drifting past a little spot where the river whirls around in an eddy, and you'll just need some extra distance to get in there.

You will also be fishing with larger flies that necessitate the turnover of a heavier rod and line. The smallest fly I used in Botswana was a size 6 Clouser Minnow. The rest are even larger and have even more wind resistance. A line weight is a powerful tool in handling these heavier flies. Furthermore, the tiger fish have incredibly sharp teeth that necessitate the use of strong and heavy leaders. Some people use steel leaders; others use heavy monofilament. However, as always, it boils down to your personal style. Peter, the photographer, used his 5-weight, which was his favorite rod. It was the only rod he needed, and he handled it very well. He might not have had an easy time if he had caught a really large tiger, but the big ones were not due for another month or so. In any case, he enjoyed using it and caught plenty of fish.

In a word, you can bring any rod you want. I think you will be more effective with the heavier ones in terms of covering a lot of water, but it is also a great deal of fun to land fish on lighter rods. Use your own judgement.

LINES AND LEADERS

The most effective all-around line I used was an intermediate. I found that the majority of the fish I caught were sub-surface, but not far under. Much of the fishing is blind casting into deep stretches of river. What I did over and over again was to throw a cast a far as possible, let it sink for a couple of feet, and then strip it back with some authority.

Another good line to have is a weight-forward floating line. This is a great line to use in the morning or in the evenings when the sun is low. You use it with popper patterns on the surface, and pull them off the lily pads. This technique inspires very aggressive takes.

The most important thing to consider in Botswana is leaders and leader management. The tiger fish have long jagged teeth that protrude out of their mouth, and they are incredibly sharp – even worse than blue fish. You will need to use steel, synthetic, or heavy monofilament leaders. Even the heavy monofilament will wear through after only a fish or two. Steel is the best material to use. Six inches of it at the tippet will be enough, but just make sure you have it.

Another peculiarity behind the tiger fishing exercise is the fly set up. We found that experimenting with secondary dropper flies was very effective. As a second leader

off the main one, it is sometimes smart to put on a smaller fly. If it looks like a bigger fly is chasing a smaller fly, the tiger fish will hit the pursuer more readily. We spent hours discussing the reasoning behind this. My conclusion was that the tiger is a predator and tries to dominate the gene pool by battling with any other predators. It is like a salmon eating the eggs of other salmon. Whatever the reason, there were certainly higher strike rates when we used the droppers. So, read up on your knots, and bring a pair of pliers to twist and turn the steel leaders.

THE FLY BOX

Tiger fish are vicious predators, and they will strike at anything that doesn't frighten them. But, of course ,it is always best to make your flies look like a tasty example of their favorite minnows.If you need the name of a good fly that you can find in the stores, it is the Lefty's Deceiver. This is essentially a normal Deceiver that has more chartreuse than white in the feathers. White and chartreuse are probably the two most effective colors you can use with these fish, making this fly especially deadly.

There is a drawback to the Deceiver – it is not weighted. Many times, we found fish sitting deep in an eddy behind a slight indent of the bank. To get at these fish, it is necessary to first cast above them, and then let the fly come down to where they can see it. To get down to these fish, a Clouser Minnow is the perfect fly. In fact, I used this fly more than any other in Botswana. The local guys like to

RIGHT: *The most charming thing about fishing in Botswana is the grand chorus of wildlife always watching from the banks. The kingfisher, pictured here, is one of the most common visitors we saw in the papyrus along the canals. They watch quietly over their brilliant red beaks and fly from branch to branch looking for food throughout the day. Sometimes, they come to rest on a crocodile's back or a hippopatamus' snout. Everyone seems to like having them around.*

tie them with very noticeable eyes. They think it triggers the hunting instinct in the fish, and they may well be right. The favorite is a Clouser tied with dark red eyes; it is called the Drunken Bastard.

When you are just fishing open water or pools, and not having to reach strategically into nooks and crannies, there is one set up that works the best. Tie a large Clouser on to the leader. Then, six inches up, drop a much smaller one off the leader. In the water, this looks like a big minnow hunting a little minnow. The tiger then feels the urge to settle the dispute by asserting his authority and killing the predatory minnow. It's all theory, but it produces results.

ABOVE: *As the sun goes down in a remote bush camp, your senses sharpen tremendously. Every noise in the darkness brings with it a moment of breathlessness. Once the stars come out, and everyone retires to their tents, however, the sounds become more familiar and a sense of peace comes over you. Closing your eyes and listening to it at night reveals a concert of music difficult to forget.*

RIGHT: *The Clouser Minnow, and variations of it, are probably the best all round flies in the Okavango. The weighted eyes help you get down to the fish, and the long, trailing bucktail moves like a live fish. White and chartreuse are good colors to start with. Just bring plenty of flies, or material to tie them with, because no fly lasts long once its been in the mouth of a tiger or two.*

ESSENTIAL KIT

Sun block is vital. You are just north of the Kalahari Desert, and it is seriously hot and sunny. You will also be out on the water all day, with the reflected light effectively doubling the exposure you get. You will want to dress scantily, so much of your body will be exposed. Bring strong block, and wear a hat.

The mosquitoes in Botswana are the size of hippopotami. They also travel in clouds. You'll learn to love your repellent, especially in the evenings when you are trying to eat. You will probably have some type of internal prophylactic for protection against malaria, but reducing your exposure to mosquitoes is always a good thing because they do carry the disease. The lodge provides a mosquito repellent spray that is unavailable in some countries, and it is almost totally effective.

You will not be doing any wading, and even if you were crazy enough to give it a try, the water is always very warm. Just wear lightweight clothes, preferably white clothes. This reduces the amount of sunlight you attract. I wore a white linen pullover all the time and found it very comfortable.

Bring some sandals; you won't be venturing into the bush very much, and will probably go barefoot on the boat during the day. A pair of hiking boots is always advisable in case you want to go for a walk anywhere. Finally, bring a good hat and a pair of sunglasses to protect your head and eyes. I wore a big straw hat all day that shaded my face, and was also very cool. Polarized lenses in your glasses are not so important, as sight fishing is very rare, but they may help with the glare.

CONSERVATION WATCH

Botswana is a country with little heavy industry and much of the terrain is still totally uninhabited. It has one of the most beautiful ecosystems that we were fortunate enough to visit anywhere on Earth. There are, however some quite serious conservation issues. In 1995–96 there was an outbreak of a severe lung disease in the cattle populations north of the capital city of Maun, and almost all of the cattle herds had to be destroyed. This caused a famine risk and a tremendous loss of jobs for the local populations who worked in the cattle industry.

In response, the country received various forms of international relief. In one instance, this relief came in the form of gill nets donated from Scandinavia. These nets were distributed amongst the local population in an effort to allow people to catch fish to make a living and, as a result, many of the cattle hands became commercial fisherman. But the commercial fishing that is now carried out with these nets along the Okavango Delta has put a tremendous amount of pressure on the local fish populations. There are currently no laws set in place to govern the size of the gill nets used, the amount of fish that can be taken, or any seasons when fishing is restricted.

One day, when we were drifting down the river, we came across some nets that had been left in the water and forgotten about. We spent over an hour hauling them out of the water. The boat consisted of me, Guy, Peter, P.J., and Beverly – all staunch conservationists. When we brought the nets from the water they were tangled and contorted with hundreds – even thousands – of dead and dying fish. This, unfortunately, occurs all up and down the Okavango Delta.

Botswana is still a very rural place, but there are close to two million people and the population is rising. If no laws are put in place to curb the practices of the commercial fishermen and to properly maintain and conserve the fish populations, a situation could easily develop like the one that is already threatening the salmon populations around the world.

In order to help or get involved, I encourage you to write a letter to the National Conservation Strategy Coordinating Agency in Botswana, a division of the National Conservation Advisory Board. Write them letters of wisdom from your experiences in conservation. Respectfully tell them the importance of catch and release, and of maintaining proper fishing seasons and regulations. The tiger fish is too unique an animal to risk.

Mushanana L. Nchunga
National Conservation Strategy
Coordinating Agency
Private Bag 0068
Gabarone, Botswana
Tel: 267-302-050
Fax: 267-302-051

AFRICAN DREAMS
SOUTH AFRICA

MOUNT ANDERSON RANCH, SOUTH AFRICA

We woke up for the sunrise, which revealed one of the most vast and ethereal landscapes I have ever seen. The valleys of the surrounding mountains looked like bowls that contained a magical mixture of wind and heavy clouds. From Mount Anderson Ranch, we drove up through the valleys to the top of the mountains, and found ourselves sitting in a world completely cut off from the one we had come from. We were above the clouds, and could see wild game in three different directions. We spent the morning photographing wildebeest, zebra, blesbok, and we even saw a few jackals and hyenas. Peter was jumpy with excitement as he crept unnoticed through the fields to get the best of the shots he wanted.

In the afternoon, we caught some small panfish in one of the dams, a sheer red rockface towering above one of the sides. It was a casual day, to get adjusted to our new bearings. Later, we photographed some more game, and then went back to the main house to fish the weirs at sunset.

LEFT: *Fly-fisherman and rainbow trout, Whiskeyspruit River, Lydenburg.*

We started fishing about two hours before sunset, and were disappointed to find ourselves unable to entice anything other than the small and impulsive baby rainbows who would nibble, nibble, and bite our dry flies with little more indication than a whisper of wind on the water. I scouted the four weirs for any large fish from a pathway up above the water, and found only a couple of larger specimens, maybe two pounds or so. I threw a Dahlberg Diver into the surface film to see if I could spark the aggressive impulses in one of them, and it worked. I landed a decent rainbow, gleaming in its young colors. As I gently released it, I noticed that the fish were relatively plump for their young age .

Now, my appetite had been whetted. I knew that there must be some nice sized fish in there since they had been seen from time to time. In every pond, in every run in every stream, there is always one monster who dwarfs his neighbors. He lies idly in the darker corners, the cool waters and abundant oxygen keeping his large body strong and fit. Reigning like kings, the largest trout are so territorial, always occupying the best holding grounds. Weathered from territorial battles in their youth, and mindful of meals that delivered a hook in their mouth, these wily old trout rest beneath ledges and overgrown banks. From here, they can watch the rest of their kingdom, learning their lessons from Mother Nature in their dimly-lit, dream-like aquatic underworld.

Peering into the water, I saw several shallow littoral zones, but passed them off as being morning territory. Along the banks on the other side, there were large patches of 4-5 foot cat tails, but the sun had just set, and I could not see through the dark reflection. Scanning back and forth, I began to get anxious that it would soon be nightfall. Although I was near the house, being outside at night in Africa can make you really aware of all the good reasons for getting back inside. Soon, it would be dark, and I knew the trout would be resting as their eyes adjusted for a half an hour or so. Then, I spotted my fish. If ever there were a throne fit for a king, it was right here – a perfectly placed ledge that provided two or three feet of ceiling over a dark cavernous hole – built for a fish as a den for a fox.

It was in the farthest corner from me, with a steep hill of grass to my rear making the back-cast difficult. I tried a cast, placing my floating minnow several feet out from the hole; that way, my back cast would be more parallel to the bank, and in less danger. I tried this cast for ten or fifteen minutes, but it just wasn't good enough; I needed to be over that hole. But it was dark now, with the furthest edge of the sky just gleaming in a dim metallic blue. I guessed my chance had passed, at

RIGHT: *Ohrigstad Reservoir is a prime watering hole for hundreds of animal species near Mount Anderson. Water is an important* *commodity in Africa. The abundance of it in this area is one of the reasons that the wildlife is so plentiful.*

least for the time being. I considered heading home with my tail between my legs and telling my friends of the fish that I had failed to catch, but that wasn't good enough. I had to make one more cast.

I paid out a few extra feet of line at my feet, and tightened the hold on my rod. I looked across to the corner where I knew my fly must go. Then, I worriedly glanced at the steep wall of grass waiting behind me like a team of vultures to steal my fly. I raised my rod tip and made a high rolling cast behind my back. But knowing my rod had not loaded well enough, I knew I would need just one more false cast – just four extra feet to get to that hole. So, with my eyes closed in fear, I made that one last back cast, just waiting for the deadly stop of line as my hook deepened into a firmly rooted flower. But it never came. With supernatural skill, the fly rose to the challenge, and sailed silently through the air without argument, as the line straightened out in front of me. Just a second of anticipation followed as I waited to see where the fly would land.

It was too far into the dark, but I heard a very sudden "plip," and I smiled as three faint circles of light crept out through the darkness. Slowly, I stripped the fly through the surface, to imitate a tiny mouse. The anticipation was unbearable. If the fly was taken, it would be an explosive take. Passing over the dark hole, the sacrificial minnow made it to the center of the dark pond, praying for the safety of the bank. But I waited. It was a very long minute, and my mind was starting to drift when, "Wham!" – the dark water exploded into a cascade of gleaming light. I quickly lifted the rod tip, and the fight was on. I loosened the drag on my reel, as it quickly began to unwind back into the far corner of the pond that once had seemed so far away. As the heavy fish struggled and pulled, I stood on the bank feeling one hundred pounds lighter knowing that this was the perfect take. After five full minutes of this glorious feeling, a four-pound rainbow was in my hands. It wasn't the biggest fish I had ever caught, but in a pond of one-pound fish, a four-pounder reigns supreme. And having craftily stolen that title for myself, I released my treasure and returned to the lodge with my head held high.

A BRIEF HISTORY

By Bob Crass, author of *Trout in South Africa*

In Africa, brown trout are native to the Atlas Mountains of Morocco, in streams that flow north to the Mediterranean Sea, but there are no indigenous salmonoids south of the Sahara. The European settlers who came to Africa in the 19th century saw rivers that seemed to match those of their homeland, and some, whose favorite recreation was fly-fishing, wondered whether it would be possible to bring trout south across the equator.

OPPOSITE: *In Africa, you never know what's behind your back. Fishing for trout in this pond at the ranch, we could hear baboons fighting on the cliffs above us. At times it became so violent and loud, we wondered if there was a small war happening that we didn't know about. Then, quite suddenly, it would stop and a peaceful quiet would settle in around us. In this place of contradictions and opposites, there is never a dull moment.*

BELOW: *Hooking into that last trout of the day is every fisherman's wish. Here, close to the Mount Anderson Ranch, beneath an African sunset, this trout sipped a small mayfly near the bank. These high-altitude ponds have an abundance of trout and insects. They like the cooler temperatures, and the weed beds along the bank have a high oxygen content.*

In South Africa, rivers that are cool and clear enough for trout can be found in mountainous regions of the Cape, north to Natal and the Eastern Transvaal, now known as Mpumalanga. Following the successful acclimatization of trout into Australia, Tasmania, and New Zealand, residents of Cape province became the first South Africans to try importing trout eggs (ova) from Britain.

A.R. CampbellJohnston brought a consignment of ova with him on the mail ship in 1875, but they were all dead on arrival. In 1884, Lachlan MacLean arranged a shipment of 20,000 ova, which arrived in Cape Town in good condition, but only three hatched and survived, and they did not breed.

The first successful introduction of trout to South Africa took place in Natal in 1890. Eight years earlier, John Clarke Parker, a farmer who had come to Natal from the north of England, had arranged for 10,000 brown trout eggs to be sent to him from Scotland. After their journey by ship, rail, and horse cart, only 18 baby fish emerged from the eggs alive, and they were too weak to survive. Another shipment the following year was a complete failure.

However, in 1889, Cecil Younge, a member of the Natal parliament, persuaded the government to provide £500 for Parker to import ova and build a small hatchery on a cool stream flowing through a forest near Balgowan, north of Pietermaritzburg. Parker put up brick supports (which are still standing to this day) on which he rested wooden troughs, each supplied with flowing water. Early March was the latest date on which the eggs could arrive, as the breeding season depended on the time of maturity of the parent fish in the Northern Hemisphere. Parker made a cooling box containing a coil of 50 feet of half-inch diameter pipe that could be surrounded by ice. When the eggs arrived by train on 8 March, 1890, 500 lb of ice was also delivered, and additional supplies were brought each day. On 10 March, the first alevins emerged from their eggs, and within two weeks, 2000 healthy young trout were beginning to feed. In early May, 1442 fry were set free in the Mooi River, the Bushman's River, and the Umgeni River. Those placed in the Mooi failed to establish a breeding population, but in both the other rivers, the fish bred and their descendants are to be caught by fly fishers to this day.

The first trout hooked by an angler in South Africa was one of 12 inches, taken by Graham Hutchinson in the stream below Parker's hatchery in April 1892. Three months later, Parker himself caught one of the original stock in the Umgeni on a March Brown fly. It weighed 2 lbs 2 oz and was 17 inches long. It was several years, however, before the success of the trout introduction could be established and no more attempts to bring trout to Natal waters were made until 1899.

Meanwhile, the Cape government began a program of trout acclimatization and appointed a professional fish culturist, Frenchman, Ernest Latour, who hatched trout from England at the site of Ohlsson's Brewery at Newlands, a suburb of Cape Town. The brewery made use of a spring of pure, cool water for beer production, and the quality of the water was favorable for trout eggs and fry. Between 1891 and 1894, Latour reared fry and stocked the Eerste, Laurens, Berg, and Breede rivers in the Western Cape. The fiery Frenchman then quarreled with the committee appointed to oversee trout acclimatization and took a position with the Frontier Acclimatization Society at Kingwilliamstown in the Eastern Cape, where he hatched imported ova in 1895 at Pirie in the foothills of the Amatola Mountains.

Latour's place in the Western Cape was taken by John L. Scott from the Solway fisheries in Scotland. He established a hatchery with government funds, at

Jonkershoek at the headwaters of the Eerste River, some 40 miles from Cape Town. Scott stripped and fertilized brown trout ova for the first time in South Africa in 1895, using fish reared from imported eggs.

Rainbow trout were successfully reared from eggs imported in 1897 from Britain, where they had already been bred for some years. Scott found a way of packing eyed ova in boxes on layers of damp moss, allowing them to be sent to distant parts of the country by mail in the cooler months, facilitating the establishment of both brown and rainbow trout as far afield as Rhodesia.

When Latour left Pirie Hatchery in 1896, A. Stenning, a professional English fish culturist, took his place and remained there until 1903. Stenning succeeded in establishing a stock of breeding fish from which he produced ova for stocking

rivers over a wide area up to the western border of Natal. His place was taken, in 1903, by F.G. Chaplin, a man with no professional training but probably South Africa's best-known propagator of trout. He moved to Jonkershoek Hatchery in 1907, where he remained as curator until 1942. He invented the highly effective Chaplin hatching box – a floating wooden frame with a hinged lid, gauze ends and bottom. This was moored in the river and eyed ova were placed on the gauze bottom, where they obtained a good supply of oxygen, as well as protection from predators. If desired, the young hatchlings could be fed for a few weeks in the container before being released into the river.

In Natal, John Parker became active in trout acclimatization once it had been proved that the initial stocking was successful. He worked without payment, but

BELOW: The Green Hills of Africa *was one of Hemingway's lesser-known works. Here, under the endless African sky, a tale of life, death, and renewal unfolds each and every day. Lions, antelope, baboons, eland, buffalo, and hyenas are all part of the cast. Looking out at the open spaces in Africa is tranquilizing, and one would never think it was anything short of paradise.*

BELOW: *In front of the Mount Anderson Ranch, the owners have set up several fishing weirs for those who want to stay close to home, or who simply can't wait for the others to get ready. The fish are smaller, but the setting in the valley is beautiful. Behind you is Mount Anderson, the tallest mountain in the country, capped with snow, and downstream the river drops down the mountain into one of the most pure water catchments in the region. Mala-Mala Game Reserves, the controlling company, bottles water from the mountain, and keeps the ranch for the owners of the company, and special guests.*

received government support for expenses. He built a small hatchery on his farm, Tetworth, a few miles from the site of the 1890 operation. From 1899 to 1907, Parker operated the hatchery, using eggs supplied from the Cape, as well as stripping his own fish reared in the ponds on Tetworth. Both brown and rainbow trout were successfully distributed to rivers along the Drakensburg.

Two more hatcheries were set up in the years after Parker ceased operations in 1907, but no serious attempt was made to breed trout artificially in Natal until 1950, when the construction of dams to create fishing ponds gave impetus to the production of hatchery trout for stocking.

When the Natal government appointed a retired schoolmaster, L.A. Day, as inland fisheries officer in 1926, he realized that the best method of establishing trout in unstocked rivers was to transfer fish from rivers with an existing population. Since breeding tends to be over-prolific in favorable sections of the river, ample young fish are often available. Day organized parties of fly fishers to

catch trout for transfer. To carry the trout that had been caught, without any handling, Day designed metal tanks, each with a removable liner of perforated zinc that could be placed in running water. As the trout were caught, they were carried in buckets and placed in the liner until the time came to transport them. Then, the whole thing, fish and all, was placed in the tank. Many streams were stocked in this way, as well as some still waters.

To the north of Natal, along the eastern edge of the Transvaal plateau, at about 5000 feet above sea level, there are streams suitable for trout. In 1915, a program began at Lydenburg to stock streams with young trout reared from eggs sent from Jonkershoek hatchery. This endeavor was enthusiastically carried forward by F.C. Braun, a German from the Black Forest. Funds for the purchase of ova were raised through subscriptions to the Lydenburg Trout Protection and Angling Society, and over a 24-year period, Braun reared and distributed over 600,000 ova.

Trout were also established in the streams of Lesotho, to the west of Natal, beginning with the transport of a dozen brown trout from the Bushman's River in Natal, using empty kerosene cans carried on the backs of mules. More recently, air transport has enabled more trout to reach the most remote areas, far from roads.

The success of trout acclimatization in South Africa has been due, in part, to laws making the capture of trout illegal, except by the use of traditional fly tackle, and this prohibition still applies to rivers that are scheduled trout waters.

THE SOUTH AFRICA EXPERIENCE

When you arrive in the Eastern Transvaal, just a few hours east of Johannesburg, you might think you were passing through the Catskill Mountains on the way to Roscoe, New York. There is a very well developed fly-fishing culture in this part of the world, much like that on the Beaverkill River. There are old shanty house stores in old towns, and a number of decent fly-shops with local experts who will slowly tell you the current scoop in the area.

We came to a ranch in the small town of Lydenberg. There are a number of excellent trout rivers here, many of them in the Mount Anderson Catchment Reserve. Mount Anderson is the tallest mountain in South Africa, and the source from which many of these rivers spring. It is thrilling to find a trout culture so far off the normal fly-fishing routes, and the surroundings are incredible.

While not being quite so savage and wild as Botswana, the Eastern Transvaal is still an African wildlife sanctuary. You may well be peacefully wading a stream when suddenly you jump out of your skin at the sound of a family of baboons heckling you from the other bank. It can be quite unsettling, but they are tremendously amusing when seen from a comfortable distance.

A simple glance over the shoulder up on the mountain is like a look through a copy of *National Geographic* magazine. We saw eleven different types of antelope along the river, including eland and kudu, red duiker and klipspringer. The most dominant predator is the leopard, which is seldom seen but is omnipresent. hunting wild pigs and anything else it can catch. And that's just on the ground.

In the air, you will find a whole other universe of life on the wing. Trent, the resident wildlife expert at Mount Anderson, has recorded the presence of more than 100 species of birds on the mountains.

On the 26th of March, 1998, I made this entry in my journal: *"There is such a strong aura of ethereal mystery that surrounds you here. Everything is so pure, it seems to sparkle. In the morning, the mist and clouds fill the valley below. Some mornings at sunrise we drive up to the ridges for pictures. Although you still cannot see more than 100 feet in front of you, the air around you glows orange and red. There are thousands of game up here, wondering what and who we are. They kick as they run, and seem to possess a wildness and virginity that we hardly understand any more."*

Here, you will be fishing small mountain streams, usually a cast length across, which are filled with rainbow trout, and a very fertile abundance of insects. There are five or six lakes on the Mount Anderson Property that contain good size fish and challenging angling, with weed beds, cattail grass, fallen trees, and deep water troughs. Just beneath the house itself is a river that has been divided into a series of weirs, each holding small fish worth casting to, and some big ones also.

Also within the Mount Anderson Water Catchment is another fishing haven worth mentioning. Highland Run is a private fishing reserve for members who build cabins and houses along the property. Douglas Starling has spent years developing and maintaining this river. Starling's work over the years has paid off, and now the river is home to an average of two- to three-pound rainbow trout. These take a fly readily, but are still wary enough to necessitate some fishing skills.

TACKLE AND GEAR
ROD AND REEL

The fishing here is simple; it is classic trout stream fishing. The fish are skittish, and the waters are calm. The best rod you can have for every situation is a 5-weight, my all-around favorite rod. It is delicate enough not to spook anything, but large enough to cover water effectively.

Another rod I would have with me is a nice, soft 3-weight. A great deal of the fishing here is at very close quarters. Particularly at the weirs behind the ranch, you will be fishing on small areas of calm water, and you will want a small rod with which you can throw light dry flies and small nymphs. Aside from that, bring whatever suits you. Everyone has a favorite rod, and some tricks up their sleeve. Most of the water here is relatively small, and you will not find any large, rushing rivers that would necessitate a large rod. Use whatever you feel comfortable with.

LINES AND LEADERS

The fishing you will be doing on the still water lakes will be mostly stationary with long, blind casts. You will want to find a nice spot, and not move too much and muddy up the water. These conditions are right for a weight-forward line, maybe one weight heavier than your rod. You will also find some rising fish, and some strategic fishing angling back in towards the bank. The weight-forward will be a good all-around line for that as well.

Down at Highland Run and Douglas Starling's other rivers, you will have a moving freestone stream much more reminiscent of a Blue Ridge Mountain trout

BELOW: I don't think any of these women fly-fish, but they can tie a perfect Royal Coachman in 30 seconds. Here, at Fishy Pete's fly factory in Lydenburg, these ladies supply an avid local and international fishing audience with thousands of flies every day. They tie everything from a spun deer hair popper on a 2 hook to a small calibaetis dry fly on a 22 hook.

stream. It will be no more than a cast length across, but will present numerous casting challenges to reach strategic spots. In these cases, I always prefer to use a double-taper line in case I need any quick roll casts at long distance, or need to pick up and load the line quickly. Most people like weight-forwards these days, but I think a double-taper, with the top five or six feet of the front taper cut off, is the best possible line for advanced casting situations.

As for leaders and tippets, just match the leader to your rod. A nine-foot leader with 4 or 5x tippet will be fine. You are not likely to see any fish much bigger than five pounds. In fact, most will be just a pound or two. Light leaders are fine.

THE FLY BOX

The fly box here is very simple. You will just want a nice selection of mayflies, caddis, and stone flies – dries and nymphs. The fly I used the most while I was there was the Adams. The fish just loved it. One time, when I had seen a fish sipping flies out of the surface film, I was casting into the bank from the middle of a pond. When I cast the fly, it looped up over a branch, and the Adams was just hanging in the air above the water. Before I could jiggle it back over, the fish came straight up out of the water and slammed it. He ended up breaking the line, but it was the most exciting take I have ever seen.

As I have said before, you will sometimes be blind casting to strategic spots in the lakes and ponds. Here it is good to have small streamers or even Wooly Buggers. Size 8 or 10 nymphs work well if you strip ever so slowly. The streamers and leaches you will want to strip with long, smooth strips, or short, jumpy strips.

ESSENTIAL KIT

At this altitude, you will be above the clouds for most of the night and morning, and it can get quite cold, so bring a sweater and some relatively warm clothes. During the day, it can get warm, but unless you go down the mountain, it usually stays pretty cool. Carry plenty of layers with you and bring a windbreaker. Also, even though the air may be cool, the sun is still strong when it comes out, especially at high altitude. So, bring some sun block if you have sensitive skin.

There is a lot to see here, and miles of space to wander, but it's important to remember that in Africa everything bites. So when you are not fishing, and you want to go off exploring, you will want a good pair of hiking boots to protect you from ground-dwelling surprises.

You will probably never see such a wide array of wildlife, mountains, and overall beauty in your life – it is absolutely incredible. So bring a camera, plenty of film, and a big lens. You could take pictures all day here.

LEFT: *We like to release all the wild fish we catch, but some of the lakes are stocked every year on Mount Anderson, so we treated ourselves to lunch in the mountains. One German judge we spoke to believed that releasing every fish reduces fishing to torture. He believed that by keeping one fish occasionally, the traditional point to fishing is maintained. This was the only trout we killed on the trip around the world. Despite any arguments, catch-and-release of all wild fish is one of the best means of ensuring a healthy fishery for the future — especially with the increased pressure they see year after year.*

CONSERVATION WATCH

The Eastern Transvaal is a remarkably diverse and unique ecosystem. The Mount Anderson Ranch is owned by Michael Rattray, under the umbrella of the Mala Mala Game Reserves, and he has taken tremendous steps toward strengthening and maintaining this valuable resource.

In the winter of 1982, the Sand River at the Mala Mala Game Reserve ran dry for the first time, sparking Michael's concern about the causes. Mining and deforestation reduce the natural filters on the mountainside, and over-grazing causes the earth to heat up, increasing evaporation. Michael Rattray's interest in these problems has led to the creation of several "water catchments" in eastern South Africa, designed to protect the water that flows from the tops of mountains.

Under normal conditions, around 80 per cent of a river's flow comes from the top 20 per cent of the mountain. When water occurs in the form of rain or melting snow in the springtime, it soaks into the ground, filters its way down the mountain, and drains out in the form of a stream or river. Proper land management maintains the sponge-like qualities of the mountain. This is a water catchment, holding the water and distributing it evenly as it feeds the rivers below.

Mala Mala has created approximately 50,000 acres of water catchments that have restored and protected the river flows going through the Kruger National Park and the areas surrounding Mount Anderson. These highly successful catchments now provide a sanctuary for clean, pure water to be used by humans and the millions of wild animals, including the fish, living in South Africa.

If you are interested in becoming involved with the Mala Mala water catchments, which are overseen by the Green Trust and the World Wildlife Federation, you can contact:
David Evans
Managing Member
Mala Mala Game Reserves
PO Box 2575
Randburg 2125, South Africa
Tel: 27-11-789-2677
Fax: 27-11-886-4382

THE RIVER IS A LADY
ARGENTINA

O'FARRELL'S LODGE, CHUBUT, PATAGONIA

It had been a long time since I last fished a big river. Last March, I spent a day on the Green River in Utah, and before that was when I was working in Montana a couple of years ago. I had spent countless hours in the saltwater with my fly rod, and hit plenty of small brooks and mountain streams. But, the stakes are higher on a big river. Quite often it demands a great deal of skill, the results are more rewarding, and it is an experience of a different kind. I had almost forgotten that feeling until I found myself once again beside that great torrent of water, this time in the mountains of Argentina.

As a kid I often spent the weekends with my friend, ankle-deep in mud along the banks of a large creek by our house in Atlanta, Georgia. We would swing from trees and jump off bridges – all for the thrill of burying ourselves completely in the cool embrace of the water. I do not think I realized it then – at least no more than my young mind would allow – but the waters were already beginning to occupy a deep and sacred place in my heart.

LEFT: *Morning mist over the Rio Grande, Patagonia, Argentina.*

As the years went by, I grew much bigger, and so did the waters that I discovered. Somewhere between the deafening rush of the Nile and the 50-foot tides in Alaska, my heart was captured, and now I, too, am haunted by waters.

For many men, there is a woman who sits at command in the throne of his heart. She has a power, at times a mischievous one, that holds sway over his thoughts, wherever he may roam. To me, she is the embodiment of a river. Steadily she pursues her course, endlessly meandering her way through the mountains that husband her. Oh, the river, she is a lady! She is beautiful enough to be the subject of myths. There is a calm glimmer in the mornings as she slowly emerges from the darkness of the night before. It is a thrill to be up before her, to look at her briefly as she sleeps, softly rolling over the glistening stones below. And just when you think all is still, the sun peeps through the trees and you see a rise 90 foot downstream. "Plip! Good morning." And with that, the day has begun.

Soon the river is alive, pouring forth with the great force of life. Her colors light up, her ripples get a little faster, and the sounds and smells become a little crisper. This is the force that measures the progress of time, that changes the course of events. She brings to the world an immortality. As long as she is there, she is forever pushing forward, always changing. She can capture your imagination and your heart like a fire, confidently stealing your whole attention as she burns with brilliant colors of passion.

It is into this incredible world of life that fly-fishing leads you. Wading away from the safety of the shore, you find yourself enveloped completely by this current of water. As the sun rises, and your line slices through the mountain air, some of God's most beautiful creatures take wing. As if guided by a gentle hand, mayflies and caddis break free of their aquatic domain. Sprouting wings, they make a dash for the heavens, like snowflakes returning to the sky. Many people will go their whole lives without ever knowing the names of these creatures; without ever seeing them lift their delicate bodies off the water's surface. To a fly-fisherman, they are like a candle illuminating a small piece of what goes on in the darkness below.

Oh! To know the mysteries that lie beneath the surface. Looking into the river's eyes can be oppressively bleak if you do not understand her. Filled with secrets and ghosts, the river is a world entirely unto its self, awesome in its scope. Water is the element from which all life began, and it surely knows the secret of the unanswerable questions that plague us all. Peering into her darkest corners and her swirling pools, I see reflections of my own life. A glimmering wave of light passes before me, and I am reminded of someone that I once loved, haunted by those that I've lost, and I search curiously for answers to the question, "Why?" She just says the answer lies within me.

But from time to time there is an echo of my admiration and respect. With a little skill and a little luck, my line is pulled below with a great strength. And, as if to congratulate me for a job well done, a secret is revealed; a rainbow leaps through the surface. Flying through the air and splashing down as I once did, it is a joy to see such life breaking out of the dark world from which it came – to be reminded that every night has its dawn, and the answer is there. Somewhere inside, it can be found. Amidst the chaos of the rapids and the collected push of the calm waters, she will continue to flow. Life gives us the opportunity to add what we may, and as the sun sets in our eyes, we can smile, knowing that it did not go unfished.

BELOW: *Part of the Andes, the Situacion mountain range towers beyond the Rio Grande valley in Patagonia. Lying on the fault line that extends from the southern tip of South America all the way up to Alaska, the Andes contain several major trout species. Introduced to Argentina in the past 150 years, they have thrived in one of the most successful wildlife acclimatization efforts in history.*

PREVIOUS PAGE: *They call the water in Argentina "gin clear." You can see to the bottom of almost every river, some of which contain the biggest trout in the world. A 10-12lb fish we saw from a bridge over the Rio Arrayanes required a long and delicate cast in order to fool him. The big ones don't grow old by being foolish: this one got away.*

BELOW:*As the mist burns off the surface of the Rio Grande, a good day of fishing gets started. As soon as the sun begins to heat the water up, insects begin to swim to the surface and hatch. It is a beautiful scene to watch the fog swirling around a fisherman casting in the morning.*

A BRIEF HISTORY

The explorations of the world, and mankind's journeys to discover and settle the farthest ends of the Earth, have captured our imagination since the time of the Vikings. The stories of Eric, Columbus, Magellan, Balboa, and thousands of others have captivated our love of adventure, and the ensuing stories of colonization have both horrified and fascinated us. These are tales of Shakespearean magnitude, complete with tragedy, legends of love, mystery, and glory.

But *Homo sapiens* is not the only species on Earth capable of capturing the imagination; salmonoids have a history of their own. Millions of trout and salmon have traveled thousands of miles to conquer and settle new territories. Many of these journeys were fated for disaster, others ended in bloodshed and the decimation of native fish species, others were lost and stranded like Robinson Crusoe. If only each fish had an identity, their history would be a voluminous work complete with the names of villains, conquerors, and heroes. One major tale of trout colonization concerns Argentina.

Many of the facts on the history of trout fishing in Argentina came from William C. Leitch's excellent book, *Argentine Trout Fishing.* I recommend the read.

Argentina has never been a British colony, but in the 19th century, the British presence was much stronger than it is now. Along with their passion for cricket and tea, English gentlemen loved trout fishing. As a result, the first attempt at introducing trout was made by an unrecorded Englishman. These first salmonoids were British rainbows (*Oncorhynchus mykiss*) and they arrived in Hurlingham, just outside Buenos Aires, in 1879. They were brought to a small stream, now unfishable, called the Arroyo Moron. Like many settlers, these fish perished in the hot summer temperatures, and did not return to this slow moving stream for over a decade.

The Argentine government later sent surveyors into the Andes to observe the natural resources of the land. The most notable of these men was Francisco "Perito" Moreno, who strongly advised introducing fish species into the highly fertile lakes and rivers of Patagonia. John Titcomb, the most widely respected fisheries biologist in the US, was given the task of introducing the fish.

Titcomb took to the task with excitement. Arriving in 1903, he set off alone on horse and wagon for a 19-day trip into the mountains to study a lake known as Lago Nahuel Huapi. He spent several weeks studying pH levels, oxygen content, water temperatures, and so on. His studies concluded that the Patagonian waters were ideal for fish, and he immediately set about building temporary wooden hatcheries beside the lake. When the hatcheries were completed, he returned to Buenos Aires to order some fish eggs from the US. His request was received by one

E. A. Tulian, who was charged with escorting the eggs to Argentina. In the course of making the arrangements, however, he discovered that no American steamships had refrigerated containers large enough to hold the delicate eggs. After a frantic week of research, he eventually discovered that he could ship them to Southampton, England, on ice. He could then transfer the eggs to English ships that had large refrigerated containers capable of keeping the eggs cool on the long trip to South America. All subsequent fish transportation had to be done in this way, which is possibly where the false rumor originated that Argentine trout descend from the British gene pool.

When they finally arrived in Buenos Aires, Tulian transferred the eggs to ox-drawn wagons for the extremely dangerous three-week trip to Lago Nahuel Huapi. To the local gauchos and native inhabitants, unaccustomed to trout introductions, the wagons must have looked like a mysterious caravan hiding government secrets in the mountains. But on March 4th, after 50 hazardous days of transportation, the secret was revealed as Titcomb and Tulian released their cargo into the hatcheries.

This shipment contained one million whitefish eggs (*Coregonus clupeaformis*), 102,700 brook trout eggs (*Salvelinus fontinalis*), 53,000 lake trout eggs (*Salvelinus namaycush*), and 50,000 landlocked Atlantic salmon eggs (*Salmo salar sebago*). The losses were remarkably low. The eggs hatched, and the fish mated, giving birth to one of the greatest trout fishing destinations on Earth.

Subsequent consignments were not always so smooth. The next shipment, containing rainbow trout (*Oncorhynchus mykiss*), was brought by another American biologist, a certain Mr Ormsby. However, this trip to Lago Nahuel Huapi was destined to doom. Unseasonal blizzards and bad roads slowed his caravan down so much that the eggs began to hatch in the containers almost 200 miles short of their destination. So, rather than lose the whole shipment, Ormsby hastily deposited the trout into various lakes en route to the hatcheries; descendants of these trout still populate some of these lakes today.

Numerous stories tell the tale of ill-fated, star-crossed fish migrations. On one occasion, a plane filled with alevins heading for the remote Lago Cardiel was forced down in the mountains. Rather than scrap the shipment of eggs, the pilot deposited them into a local lake, where they survived and thrived with tremendous resilience. As a result of events like these, trout and other fish have been living the life of luxury ever since throughout Argentina – even making it as far south as Tierra del Fuego, where the fabled sea-run browns can reach 30 pounds.

RIGHT: *Fishing is very much a part of the local culture in Argentina. These young boys are fortunate enough to grow up in one of the best fishing regions of the world, and they make do with whatever fishing equipment they can put together. These tin can reels will teach a child the true meaning of working for a fish if they catch a big one here on the Rio Percey, in Patagonia.*

The first decade of the 20th century saw numerous additional shipments that included most species of trout, and both Pacific and Atlantic salmon. These fish were deposited all over Patagonia, most of them successfully, some not. In 1910, these shipments ended and the birth of Argentine fly-fishing was complete. Today it is one of the greatest fly-fishing destinations on Earth, and the numbers of trout I saw there were far above anywhere else I have seen in the world. Sometimes, I felt as though I had died and woken up in trout heaven.

It is important to remember, however, that no interference with Nature is done without consequences. The trout in Argentina are thriving, but it was not without cost to the indigenous fish species. Salmonoids can be very aggressive animals – they eat each other's eggs to promote their own genetic strains, and they compete violently with other fish for territory and food. Some of the native fish could not compete with the introduced trout; the latter eventually decimated many species. The main victim has been the trucha criolla (*Percichthys trucha*), which is essentially like a species of perch that can reach in excess of six pounds. It looks like a black bass, and has very sharp dorsal and pectoral fins. Other victims

BELOW: *In the Rio Arrayanes, this rainbow trout feeds near some very lush beds of grass. Trout like underwater vegetation because it supplies a good deal of oxygen, and supports an abundant insect population in most cases. Sometimes it's fun to just watch them feed for a while. It can give you a good idea as to what they are eating.*

have included the Patagonian kingfish, the pejerrey, and the peladilla. Although these fish still survive in places where the trout cannot go, their numbers have dwindled drastically. The decline of these and other native Patagonian fish species is the high price paid for the fishing opportunities on offer today.

As unfortunate as the loss of these native fish may be, it has to be said that fly-fishing in Argentina is one of the greatest experiences any fly-fisherman can have. Families of gauchos still drive cattle through the mountains, roe deer and large rabbits color every day; and the rivers you'll be fishing will be teeming with large rainbows and brown trout swimming through thousands of miles of the cleanest, most pure blue water you could ever imagine.

So, when you go there, bring your favorite rod and reel, and be prepared to discover a true haven. You can fish the famous rivers, or you can be adventurous and explore the unknown. Martin O'Farrell, our guide and host while we were there, took us to his best-kept secret (I promised not to tell where). Surrounded by the most poignantly beautiful place we saw on the trip, we spent the afternoon catching large four- to seven-pound brook trout that were coming up a river to spawn. Red as an African sunset, they were only one of the many great secrets this country has to offer.

THE ARGENTINA EXPERIENCE

In the course of our travels, Argentina was without a doubt one of the very top fly-fishing destinations we went to anywhere in the world. We fished in Patagonia, which combines the best of every aspect of the fly-fishing tradition. The rivers are spectacular. Most of them are classic freestone streams filled with water so pure you can almost always see right to the bottom. Many of these rivers were so large that

we floated them in rafts, fishing along the way, and stopping from time to time to wade. Rafting also helps to cover the many miles of water there is to fish. We fished the Rio Rivadavia and the Rio Grande in this fashion. Both of these rivers are very exotic, large freestone streams. We ended up fishing four different sections of these two rivers, and we could easily have visited a dozen more. Martin O'Farrell's little secret turned out to be the best fishing spot on the whole trip. I'm sworn to secrecy, so I cannot divulge its whereabouts, but a polite enquiry will get any guest of his lodge a special trip to this treasure chest of large brookies and rainbow trout.

Argentina, however, is not limited to freestone streams. We fished a small chalk stream called the Spring Creek, or Arroyo Piscada, which was very slow and shallow. We were sight fishing for two-pound rainbows, and here we needed a 7x tippet and small midge flies, called "Brassies," that have to be delivered in the surface film right over the fish's nose. It was tremendous fun, and called into play all of the skills one could muster. On one bank of this river stands an old gravestone marking the death of a man shot by Butch Cassidy.

Many of the large rivers in Patagonia flow into and out of great stillwater lakes, such as Lago Bueno. These lakes can be fished in many ways. The easiest is with long casts and streamers or minnow patterns. Martin preferred the challenge of throwing dry flies on the edges of weed beds and large rocks. I preferred using an intermediate line with mayfly nymph patterns, to catch the larger fish. You must strip very slowly as if the nymph is angling up from the bottom.

The fishing experience as a whole will be one of the best of your life. The famous "gin clear" water will haunt your memories. The abundance of fish is astounding, and if you watch carefully, you may well see a few fish over ten pounds.

And, of course, more than anything else, the experience is colored by the people. Argentines are an extremely sociable lot. As a man, you should be prepared to give a woman a kiss on the cheek when you meet her formally, as it is a custom in Patagonia. It is not a necessity, but you will only remind them you are a visitor if you do not. Also, be prepared to eat well. The Argentines like to include their famous beef with any meal they can, even if it's first thing in the morning. You'll need to get used to a different sense of time, too. In Buenos Aires, most of the restaurants didn't really start to fill up until 9.30 or 10.00 at night. Throughout Argentina, the good times drag on late into the night and every day after lunch you can expect everyone to take a little siesta. It is an incredibly pleasant way to spend a fishing trip, and one you're sure to enjoy.

LEFT: *The glorious expanses and wide Patagonian rivers are the perfect setting to open up with some long casts. This fisherman didn't have the longest cast we saw on the trip, but it was pretty good.*

He is fishing the Rio Grande, which flows straight into Chile. One day, I was floating the river by myself, missed the take out spot, and passed right into the next country without my passport.

ABOVE: *A rainbow finds shelter beneath the branch of a beautiful lenga tree in the Rio Rivadavia. Fish will quite often rest near the banks of a river. Sometimes, they even sleep.*

When approaching a body of water, it is always best to carefully scout the edges first or even make a few blind casts to nice spots. The best fish may be waiting in the shadows.

TACKLE AND GEAR

ROD AND REEL

Your choice of these is largely dependent on your personal preferences, but before deciding, it is important to know exactly where you will be going and what you will be fishing for. Argentina offers everything from small brook trout to Atlantic salmon, and even a few elusive Pacific salmon coming up from Chile.

The best all-around rod that I would recommend is a 9-foot 5-weight. With this, you can fish both the large and small rivers. A lot of the fishing is done with dry-flies and droppers from a raft. In this situation, you won't need too much distance, so a 5-weight is both powerful and delicate enough.

However, if you want to experiment, bring an array of rods. Some of the rivers can be very large, so it could be fun to bring a larger 7- or 8-weight rod to throw long casts with large streamers and strip them across. Or, you could be on a much smaller chalk stream. I used my Winston 3-weight to cast midges in a shallow brook no more than 15 feet wide. I would not have wanted anything bigger. It never hurts to have options. However, you will get into fish no matter what. Just remember that this is one of the world's greatest destinations. You may even become religious about it, so bring your favorite rod.

LINES AND LEADERS

If you can cast a double-tapered line as far as you can a weight-forward, I always recommend a double taper for this type of fishing. A double-taper will offer you greater line control at longer distances, and roll casting may make things easier with all of the trees in the mountains. That is my preference. Most people, it seems, prefer a weight-forward line. This does have some great advantages. With very little effort, you can shoot line considerable distances. Weight-forwards also load the rod quite quickly, and this helps when you are rafting. If you are passing by a spot

BELOW: *Rainbow trout feeding in the Rio Rivadavia. This was one of the cleanest and clearest rivers we have seen anywhere in the world, and the colors of the water are reminiscent of the Caribbean. But clear water is an advantage for predators like eagles and other birds of prey, which is why many trout like to feed beneath a structure like this fallen tree.*

BELOW: *Cattle ranches are still a way of life for many gauchos in Patagonia. These three boys with their father look like characters from an old Western. But, there is no TV in their house; they live in a small log cabin beside the river. The boy on the right had recently caught a king salmon from the Rio Grande.*

Apparently, there are still some Pacific salmon that swim from the ocean in Chile all the way up the river into Argentina to spawn.

where you have just seen a rise, you will want to pick up quickly and redirect your line immediately before you drift by and miss the opportunity.

For Patagonia, bring a full array of leaders and tippet material. I used everything from 2x using streamers and leach patterns to 7x on the smaller streams when there was no wind. There can be a great deal of wind, though, so bring some thicker diameter end lines. You may also catch some very large fish, so be ready. I fished with 5x almost every day. I like being invisible, and I actually went through a whole spool of it during our stay because I like to retie all my leaders in the morning. You are certain to be doing a lot of fishing, so be sure not to run out of your preferred tippet material.

THE FLY BOX

In many ways, Patagonia is a lot like the American West – Colorado or Montana. The flies you will use are mostly the same, as well. Ask your hosts about what kind of hatches to expect during the time you will be visiting.

The fishing we did was mostly dry fly with a nymph dropper. If I cast my mind back to the rig my guides preferred more than any other, I would think of a large, highly visible Royal Wulff, with a size 14 bead-headed pheasant tail dropper. The bead head makes your nymph look like it's riding an oxygen bubble to the surface. But rather than sound like we really know what we are doing, let's just say it just attracts the fish more. The dry fly acts as both an indicator for the nymph,

and a dry fly option for the fish. If you like doing this, using a large Royal Wulff or Humpy is best to provide the visibility you may need.

If you want to get a little more professional, bring a nice box of flies. Most types of mayfly nymphs will work well. I like Hare's Ear nymphs; they have a great texture to them that looks very realistic. You will also find quiet water with rising trout, and you can spot some of them cruising over the grass or weed beds. Bring some dries for them to see. A Parachute Adams, or a Flying Ant will never hurt. Also, leach patterns such as Wooly Buggers, or streamers will help you cover a lot of water in the big sections or in lakes.

Argentina has beautiful hatches of all types of mayflies. Sometimes, they look like snow rising off the water. My favorite thing to do is bring my little fly-tying kit. Whenever the group takes a break, I set it up on a branch or root or the strangest place possible and tie whatever the day is inspiring me to tie. It may seem like a lot of work, but it really gets you into the zone.

ESSENTIAL KIT

Polarized glasses are a must. You may not always use them, but without them you are blind. You will not very often get the opportunity to look into water as clear as this, especially when it is filled with so many fish. So, enjoy it.

When we were there, the weather was very cold in the mornings, but by midday we would sometimes be sweltering in the sun. Be prepared to wear layers. In the Andes, weather patterns can change quickly. You may experience hot and dry, then cold and wet in the same day. It may not be too easy on your suitcase, but just bring one good raincoat, a good fleece, and a few flannel shirts to help regulate your body with the changing temperatures.

The altitude is considerable, and during a good part of the season the water will be cold, so bring your waders. Everybody says neoprene will keep you warm, but I don't think anything can beat Gore-Tex with sweatpants underneath.

The bugs were not too bad when we were there, but I have heard they can be terrible. Sometimes, the midges can be annoying, especially if you pass through a whole cloud of them. Just bring some good bug dope, and be careful not to get it on your flies. Trout are very sensitive and can smell the stuff in the water.

Aside from that, just remember the usual. You may want a net in case you catch a monster. Hemostats are very important. Trout are a very delicate fish, so always pinch the barbs and get the hook out of their mouth as quickly as possible.

LEFT: *Argentine beef is some of the best in the world. Until these cattle fatten up, the gauchos will herd them from pasture to pasture in search of the best grazing. Here, near Trevelin,* *they drive the herd through a river to bring them closer to home. The boy in the black cape, whom we called Zorro, handled his whip like a true master.*

CONSERVATION WATCH

Argentina is a unique country in many ways. From Buenos Aires to Patagonia, to the harsh coasts of Tierra del Fuego, each region has its own identity and character. One of the most outstanding aspects of Argentina is its pristine landscape. It is an absolutely flawless ecosystem with an abundance of natural resources.

In the early years of the 20th century, prospectors and settlers began to move into the Patagonian region. In 1902, Karl Wiederhold and Fritz Hube, two German settlers moved into Bariloche and began chopping down trees and exporting timber to Europe. This started a long and sustained interest in the mining and mineral rights of the relatively untouched Patagonian landscapes. As forests began to disappear, regulating the timber industry became an issue.

In 1934, the first railroad connecting Buenos Aires and Bariloche was completed. That same year saw the creation of the Commission Pro Naçional

RIGHT: It is a custom in Argentina that everyone takes a one-hour siesta after lunch. Dinners are served much later, and red wine comes with lunch. While everyone slept, I tied flies beside the Rio Rivadavia to refill my fly box. Everyday, the trout are interested in something a little different; so it's fun to bring along a travelling vice in order to match the hatch.

Parques, with Exequiel Bustillo as the first Chairman of the Board of Directors. He understood the need for businesses and the environment to find a way to evolve together. His primary concern was protecting Argentina's natural resources, but he also wanted the locals to live off the land and find a self-sustaining way to use the country's resources. The Commission worked with many businesses and organizations on both a national and a local level to accomplish this aim.

Argentina has been able to prosper, but retain its pristine landscape. This is primarily through the development of ecotourism, a concept developed by Arthur Oyola-Yemaiel. Traveling fishermen, explorers, and general outdoorsmen contribute a great deal to the local economies today. This dependency on ecotourists spearheads the country's conservation efforts.

Argentina does still have problems with business interests threatening the environment. Some years ago, a power company built a large hydroelectric dam in southern Chubut. The dam flooded a large valley and destroyed tens of thousands of trees. Today, many of these trees still stand, but it is like a graveyard, the trees are all dead and gray. From a boat you can look down through the water at the tops of trees a hundred foot tall. The power company never arranged for a timber company to remove the trees and put them to good use. Many of them got caught up in the dam; others just floated away.

Although much of the Andes are protected by National Forest laws, it is still important to be responsible each and every day. This is not something that can be accomplished by one person individually, but by all naturalists working together. One of the greatest ways tourists to the region can protect the countryside is by being responsible fishermen and naturalists. Make a presence by bringing friends and family. Keep the country welcoming to tourists interested in the environment. If the country loses that, the forests could be threatened commercially.

If you are interested in Argentine Conservation efforts, contact:
Administration de Parques Nacionales
Av. Sante Fe 690
Capital Federal (1059)
Buenos Aires
Argentina

For information about local parks in Patagonia, contact:
Parque Nacional Los Alerces
9201 Villa Futalaufquen
Chubut
Argentina

PERFECTION WAS TODAY
NEW ZEALAND

MOTUEKA RIVER LODGE, MOTUEKA

I caught a fish today. Every time I think about it, it brings another smile to my face. The fishing in New Zealand brings back to me that exhilarating feeling I once had as a small boy when I caught my first bream from the creek in my front yard at home. New Zealand returns you to the absolute purity of fly fishing. It contains every element – from the sights and sounds, to the pounding heart and the concentration of a stalking tiger – of when I first began.

Images of my first time fishing flow about my head. They are all melted together by the passage of time, but I can remember the water, the garter snakes swimming from one bank to the other, the sun shining, and the excitement. It was a time when I did not know or understand the morals of moderation. I had absolutely no scruples whatsoever about digging up the biggest, juiciest earthworm in Georgia, and watching with pleasure as it kicked about on my hook. I did not care what else was happening in the world. At that moment, nothing was more important than what was going on in the dark waters below. If the line so much

LEFT: *Karamea River, South Island, New Zealand.*

as quivered, my heart would reach through my chest and send electric shocks down my arms as I set the hook into the mouth of the luckiest fish on Earth. What bream wouldn't yearn to be yanked out of the water by a being a hundred times its size? As it struggled to free the metal hook from its mouth, I would tear across the yard at full steam like a messenger bringing presents to the king. Desperate for someone to acknowledge the enormity of what I had just accomplished, I broke through the door of my house proudly displaying the half-suffocated fish with its eyes wide open, and its lips puckering frantically for air. Yet, as if the plague had just arrived, my mother and sister would swiftly back away from me. My excitement would soon change to fear as my mother yelled across her pointed finger, "Alexander, you get that fish out of here!"

I had to accept that fishing would be a world of my own; an excitement that I would harness alone. It was a thrill that I was dedicated to physically and mentally. Imagine the thrill of discovering for the first time that out of a pool of water – tranquilizing in its depth and beauty – could come a wild fish. I discovered through the years how to throw a fly, and if I could make it stand on the water's surface ever so gently, the entire world beneath me, dark and fluid, would rise with a sudden splash, and out of the darkness would come light. I became a dreamer. I always look for the answer around the corner, the one not readily apparent. My search stems from the belief that perfection in life is not something that you will find sitting on your doorstep. It is a style of living, one that is punctuated by magical moments when your soul is warmed by the smile of knowing that you have created art from life.

Stalking brown trout is New Zealand's answer to perfection. You should only come here if you really love all of the many faces of fly fishing. I am no old timer, but I can tell that our ability to travel farther and faster, and the vast improvement in the world of fly fishing hardware, has spoiled us somewhat. Sometimes it makes us forget the joys of really working for a fish. That one fantastic fish. Travel has allowed me to pull out 50 sockeyes from an Alaskan river, and one day I may do the same in Russia. At the same time, I have seen people who have never fished before catch trophy trout at well orchestrated fishing clubs.

The fishing here sits on a peak above all the others. In the mornings, as we stand by the misty river preparing our gear, there is a great deal of care taken to ensure that everything is in order. I cut my leader and re-tie all my knots; I precisely align all of my guides like rifle sights, and I polish my polarized lenses to look up the half-lit valley still resting under the patches of swirling mist. The rivers here are painted with the serene beauty of perfection. And your mind sits enveloped by it all, knowing that all of your days of fly fishing up to this point have only been in preparation for this one day.

Somewhere out there, underneath the tumbling eddies of water, is the reflection of an unseen side of you. It is an animal perfectly suited to its environment, absolutely pure in its existence. As water slides by, endlessly conditioning its muscles and skin, the brown trout looms in a world made captivating by its existence. People like me travel thousands of miles under the duress of its pull. And beneath our world of dreams and hope, the famous fish devours its prey. Concerned only with survival, he is completely oblivious to the preparations and anticipation with which we bind ourselves to him. But he is prepared, and will not allow a mistake. So fishing here fills the angler with caution and respect. In most instances, we get only one chance. If you blow it, it will be gone. Looking for the discreet brown slivers of light, you might call it ghost hunting, for these trout are as elusive and difficult to spot as a ghost.

BELOW: *The brown trout in South Island rivers, such as the Motueka River, are one of the greatest fishing challenges in the world. We never blind fished a run or pockets of nice water. We would hike, and the New Zealanders would spot them in front of rocks, or feeding close to the bank. Then you have to stalk them by slipping in quietly behind them and deliver the flies without spooking them. It was heaven.*

So, with careful steps, you creep up to the water's edge and peer in. In many instances, you see only suggestions of shape and color that float over rocks, gently swaying from side to side in an uneven world of moving camouflage.

I saw one today after a couple of miles of walking. You know you're in big country when you never see a small fish. Every fish I had seen was over three pounds – most were around five or six. This one was a seven-pound female sitting like a queen in a world all by herself. Crouching by the bank, I watched her with awe, and dreamed of her capture. In this strange world, where sound is translated into shock waves of alarm, my feet were like a bull's hooves in a glass museum, and I had to tame them to keep from breaking the fragile peace. But I got into position downstream, and I threw a mayfly above her head. All I remember is the sight of her pointed nose slipping upward through the water, and then she was gone. I lifted my rod tip and she answered with a pull – a violent pull. My reel woke up with a zing, and I came back to the world with a fish on the line. I had stalked my first brown trout in New Zealand. She shone in my hands under the water, and her touch was unlike anything I can remember.

I am still a dreamer, and simple moments like this are enough to bring back the excitement I harnessed as a child. I sat beside the water, I released a seven-pound brown trout and my friends smiled as honestly as I did. Insects took to the air, and beneath God's great sky, we pushed on up the river in search of another precious piece of it all. Perfection was today.

THE SOUTH ISLAND

A BRIEF HISTORY

Despite the fact that the brown trout (*Salmo trutta*) enjoys an incredibly graceful existence throughout the southern Alps of New Zealand, the fish did not arrive here with any degree of decorum. In fact, much as in Argentina, acclimatizing the first trout into this incredibly fertile country came with a great deal of hardship and tremendous losses. The first brown trout to arrive in New Zealand were brought, in 1864, by one Alec Johnson. These fish were taken as fingerlings from the River Wey in England, and transported by sea, via Cape Horn, to Christchurch. Unfortunately, they were all dead on arrival, as the rough passage had proved too stressful for the young salmonoids.

As a result, the Southland and Canterbury Provincial Councils, which were sponsoring the acclimatization efforts, decided to halt any further importation until they had first monitored the efforts being made by British fish culturists to import fish into Australia and Tasmania.

In Tasmania, after some ten years of failures, the colonists had finally succeeded in bringing trout to these southern latitudes in 1864. They had found that by packing the fish as unborn ova on ice, rather than as hatched fingerlings, they could retard the growth rate of the fish and keep them stabilized over long periods of time. Very little care was then needed during transportation.

There was great competition between various biologists to be recognized as the first successful importers of the fish. The four greatest rivals were Frank Buckland, Francis Francis, E.H. Moscrop, and James Youl. No consensus has been able to unearth who was most responsible for introducing the fish to Tasmania, but it is reasonable to say that each of the four men made a significant contribution.

The trout that did finally make it were a mixed group of fish from England. Buckland stripped 1000 ova from stream browns collected from the Itchen River, in Hampshire. Francis then took 2000 ova from the Rivers Wey and Wycombe; these latter fish were of a sea migratory stock, and are of a different subspecies.

ABOVE: *A nice brown trout stalked and caught in the Karamea River on the South Island. Many brown trout like to feed in front of large rocks rather than behind them, as rainbows often prefer. This brown took to a red-bellied humpy on the surface. Landing a fish like this on a big river like the Karamea can be difficult with the strong current and a lot of rocks. A fisherman will often find ways of crossing quickly in places he might never otherwise go, just to get closer to a running fish.*

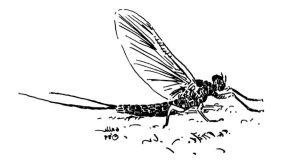

As the New Zealand fishing societies watched with interest, they began to learn how to transport trout over long distances. Packing the ova on ice was much more reliable and cheaper than any other method. They began to rebuild their trout hatcheries and prepare for another effort.

In 1866, the Tasmanian Salmon Commission offered the Canterbury Society in New Zealand a free batch of brown trout ova. The following year, Alec Johnson, who was by now the curator of the Canterbury Society, was sent to Hobart to get the ova. The fish he brought back were in poor condition from the rough passage across the Tasman Sea. Furthermore, the water temperatures at the new hatcheries proved to be too high, and all but three of the trout died. The precious survivors were carefully reared to maturity, only to be lost when the hatcheries overflowed during a flood. A rescue operation ensued for the lost fish. Luckily, two trout were finally recaptured, and returned to Mr Johnson's loving care. By a wild stroke of luck, the fish they captured were a male and female. Their offspring were stripped of their ova, which were then fertilized, and these fish became the Adam and Eve of hundreds of thousands of subsequent New Zealand brown trout.

The first trout licenses were issued in 1874 – 37 of them, to be exact – for the price of £1, and the first ever legally caught trout was landed on the opening day by a Mr A. C. Begg. By 1883, there was already talk of a 52-lb fish taking the hook. The legends of New Zealand had begun.

THE SOUTH ISLAND EXPERIENCE

Stalking wild brown trout on the South Island is the greatest fly-fishing experience I have ever had. When Carolus Linnaeus classified the *salmo trutta trutta* in 1758, he did so with no knowledge of the theories of evolution. He believed these creatures were created directly by God. In the case of these brown trout, I have to agree with him. The fishing here is raw and unadulterated. The South Island is pure fishing, with no distractions, and it calls into play every skill you have as a fly-fisherman.

We stayed at the Motueka River Lodge, Motueka. The Motueka River flows by right outside the front window, but most of the great fishing is in the backcountry. The only river we drove to was the Riwaka, a fantastic trout river that we fished the first day. Every other river we fished was a helicopter fly-out. This is what characterizes fishing here. You get your favorite rod and reel, and everything else you need, and load up in a helicopter to get airlifted to the battleground for the day. They put you down right on the banks of the river. Then you watch the helicopter take off and just squeeze its way up through the trees. Before you know it, everything is totally silent. You set everything down, and get started.

RIGHT: *The best way to access many of the best rivers is by helicopter. Landing here, on the Crow River, there was not much room, but these are the bush pilots of New Zealand. With so many rivers to fly out to, you never see another person, and you find yourself in the most pristine fisheries on Earth.*

PREVIOUS PAGE: *The Tongarirro River is one of the best in New Zealand. Some people were concerned that after the eruption of a volcano several years ago, the ash would ruin the fishing. The rocks were slightly discolored, but the fishing was some of the best we found anywhere.*

Everything has to be perfect for these fish. You have to spot them, and you only see one at a time. With very carefully trained eyes, the guide will pick out a fish, usually sitting in front of a rock, feeding. You watch for a while to see if the fish is nymphing or coming to the surface to feed. Once you know the answer, you tie on a fly and begin.

These are the most difficult trout in the world to catch. They are very wise and calculating. One false move, and your prey will be gone. You step in behind it, and with a long leader you put the fly right in front of its nose and let it drift past the fish. If the fly looks good, it will take it. If not, change flies. This is how it goes until you either catch it or spook it. Here, you never blind cast into a run or pool in the hopes of finding a fish. You walk until you spot one, usually in an uneven area of water with big rocks. Then you get set up and cast to that one fish only. In this type of fishing, every sense in your body is focused on that one object feeding in the water. If it moves at all, you hold your breath.

The beauty of the fish here is that even if you only catch one fish, it will be the catch of your life. We never caught one weighing less than three pounds.

TACKLE AND GEAR

ROD AND REEL

I used one rod the whole time I was there. I fished with my G. Loomis GLX 5-weight. It was, for me the ultimate South Island rod. It is delicate, yet powerful and accurate – the qualities you need.

These fish are very large, but you are still just fishing relatively small trout streams and rivers such as the Crow and the Wangapeka. You won't want to bring anything larger than a 5-weight. At the same time, you won't want to go any lighter than that either, because when that fish feels the tug of the line in his mouth, he will be gone in no time. So get ready for the fight of a lifetime. I hooked one particularly large fish that took me well into my backing before wrapping the line around a huge boulder and breaking off. Make sure you have 150 yards of backing, just in case. This is where you might catch The Big One.

LINES AND LEADERS

All of the casts you make to these fish will be one-time casts with tremendous deliberation. You will make one cast, and hope he takes. If not, you will wait a moment and make a second cast, and so on. With this type of fishing, you will want to use a weight forward, floating line. This will give you the punch you want to lay cast after cast onto a very small target. Most of the time, these will come from downstream of the fish. You will be casting over its head from behind, and this is very dangerous, as they are spooky. If they see your fly line, the game is up. So, you have to use a very long leader of 12–15 foot – the longer the better. The clear leader material can still spook them, but not as easily as the fly line.

THE FLY BOX

Again, the choice of flies must be very exact, as these fish are very wise. Over and over I have watched them approach the fly, inspect for a good while, and then reject it. You must give them the right fly. After you spot the fish, watch how it is feeding, and then look for clues as to what it is eating. New Zealand has many specialized flies that you will not see anywhere else.

My favorite and most effective New Zealand fly was the Dad's Favorite. This is a small brown mayfly imitation. The body is tied with brown duck quill delicately wrapped around the shank. This was the fly they were taking most while I was there, but they also take a great many nymphs. Hare's Ear nymphs were very

BELOW: *Tony Hayes, the proprietor of Tongarirro Lodge near Lake Taupo, changes flies. Coming into Tongarirro, there is a sign that reads "The Trout Fishing Capital of the World." Tony was nice enough to take us around to all of the secret spots. I caught the biggest fish of the trip in Tongarirro – a nice spawning rainbow – with Mike, one of Tony's best guides.*

effective in light cahill, brown, and green. Make some of them heavily weighted –
sometimes you will have very little space in which to land a fly, because there are a
lot of large rocks. So, when it lands, you will want the fly to sink fast and get down
to the fish before it passes. We found it very effective to use a Humpy or Royal
Wulff as an indicator. Many times, the fish will just impulsively slam the indicator.

In addition to these, bring a wide variety of all types of insects – most
specifically stoneflies, mayflies, and some caddis. But the local guides will usually
have tried and proven fly patterns for the rivers they take you to.

ESSENTIAL KIT

Polarized sunglasses will be the single most important thing you can bring to the
South Island. This is your only connection to catching fish, unless you want to rely
on the guides. There is no blind casting in many of the mountain streams.
Bug spray. There are a great many midges here, so bring something to protect
yourself. The locals seem to prefer the netted hoods that hang over their heads.

Remember to bring extra leader material, as they must be long. And re-tie
them every day. You may catch that one big fish here, so make everything perfect.

BELOW: *We found the brown
trout on the South Island to be
some of the most acrobatic of any
trout we found anywhere. When
a large trout jumps, like this one
on the Crow River, it is vital
to lower the tip of the rod. This
momentarily releases tension on
the line so a fish cannot snap it
with its tail. They call this
motion "bowing to the king."*

THE NORTH ISLAND

A BRIEF HISTORY

The North Island of New Zealand is famous throughout the world as one of the finest rainbow trout (*Oncorhynchus mykiss*) fisheries in existence.

The rainbows were not the first to arrive, however, as various acclimatization societies on the South Island had made generous donations of brown trout first, and the Auckland Society had already imported their own browns to the island. Today, however, the main attraction on the North Island is certainly the giant rainbows that can be found swimming in the streams and rivers that flow into the lakes of the Rotoiti, Rotoroa, Tarawera, and the Taupo.

In April 1883, 5000 rainbow fry arrived from the United States. These Californian trout were hatched successfully, and were reared by the Auckland Society in a series of several ponds just outside the capital city.

Upon their arrival, these pioneer fish were marked down as brook trout (*Salvelinus fontinalis*) by the Society. However, as they grew to maturity, it became clear that the fish were not brookies. An investigation to discover their true identity followed. Thomas Cheesman, a biologist at the Auckland Society, noted that the shipment of ova had been packed in California by a Mr A. V. LaMotte. Inquiries revealed that LaMotte owned and operated a hatchery of rainbow trout on Gibson Creek, a tributary of the Russian River. This gave rise to the false belief that New Zealand rainbows descended from the fish in the Russian River. It was not until well into the 20th century that the mistake was revealed and corrected.

In 1926, the Hawke's Bay Society sent specimens of trout to Stanford University to be analyzed by salmonoid biologist J. O. Snyder. Snyder found that the fish he received were steelhead trout (*Oncorhynchus mykiss irideus*), not ordinary rainbows.

As LaMotte in California handled steelhead trout, this closed the door to the mystery for many more years. However, in 1976, author Rex Forrester traveled to California. He found that a further investigation into the origins of these fish was being conducted by J.C. Frasier, regional manager of the California Fish and Game Department, Dr D. Scott of the University of Otago, New Zealand, and John Hewitson of California. The results of this investigation showed that the first rainbow trout in New Zealand's North Island were descended from a stock of trout in the Sonoma Creek – a small stream that flows directly into San Francisco Harbour. Mr Frasier wrote a letter to Mr. Forrester stating:

"A.V. LaMotte, whose name is associated with the 1883 shipment in the New Zealand Records, had operated a fish hatchery on Gibson Creek, near the Russian River at Ukiah. I am confident that this gave rise to the mistaken belief that the 1883 eggs came from the Russian River. However, LaMotte did not start to operate the Gibson Creek hatchery until 1897. The 1883 eggs came from Sonoma Creek, a stream directly tributary to San Francisco Bay where the same A.V. LaMotte operated a fish hatchery from 1878 to at least 1890. I am convinced that the chances of the 1883 eggs coming from the Russian River are negligible…The 1883 eggs were most likely shipped directly by train and boat from Sonoma to San Francisco where they were transferred to the ship embarking for New Zealand. Sonoma Creek steelheads were, with little doubt, the origin of the 1883 eggs."

It is interesting to trace back the genealogy of these fish and discover that the eggs of some trout in California gave birth to the bulk of an entire fishing empire thousands of miles away across the open sea. Today, these steelhead descendants do not make their spawning runs from the ocean into the rivers; they make their runs from the large North Island lakes. In fact, it has been discovered that the steelheads released into rivers tributary to the oceans have almost never returned to spawn – most have disappeared, presumably devoured by the larger fish in the sea.

However, the large fish that we find in Lake Taupo, and Rotorua, and even the most remote lakes and streams in the country are perfectly acclimatized. The New Zealand wildlife community has proven, over the last century, to be enthusiastic distributors of these beautiful fish. The trout have been spread by backpackers and dropped from flying planes into virtually every stretch of fishable water in the country.

Today, the descendants of those steelheads treat the lakes as their oceans. They make blistering spawning runs en masse from March onward, but mostly from July through October. The heads of these stunning fish are a deep, luminescent red, and their bodies are silver, like a fish straight from the ocean. They give the fisheries here in New Zealand a royal status amongst fly-fisherman worldwide, and prove the benefits of decades of hard work by New Zealand's acclimatization societies.

THE NORTH ISLAND EXPERIENCE

Once you move north in New Zealand to this upper island, the character of the fishing changes altogether. This is because the fishing here is generally for rainbow trout (*Oncorhynchus mykiss*). These fish behave in a different fashion altogether. They prefer different lies and they feed differently. Even so, this is still one of the finest places to fish in the world.

Rainbows thrive on the North Island primarily because of the abundance of large lakes. The rainbow is a fish that enjoys feeding in a pool more than around a large rock. They are at their best when they have a large lake in which to live, and a nice river to swim up when they spawn. This makes the North Island an almost perfect habitat for the rainbows.

The largest lake in this part of the world is called Lake Taupo, right in the middle of the North Island. There are also other famous lakes such as the Rotoroa, the Rotoaira, the Wairarapa, and the Tarawera – which is rumored to have the largest average fish size in the world. The trout run from 4 to 13 pounds, but can be difficult to catch until they gather at the river mouths to spawn.

We fished mostly in the rivers around the Taupo area. Although these are normal rainbow trout rivers, the fish look and act more like steelheads (*Oncorhynchus mykiss irideus*). They do not make runs to the sea; they spend most of the year in the lakes before spawning in the rivers where they become targets for the fly angler.

When they are coming up rivers such as the Tongariro and the Tauranga, they do not take the typical trout fly. You fish for them as you would salmon. You cast a

BELOW: *Stalking brown trout is a delicate business. When you see a big one, it is sometimes best to just sit and watch for a while. Observing the fish before you cast to it will give you an idea of what type of feeding it's doing.*

If you see them sip a fly from the surface, it is incredibly exciting, because there is no greater thrill than catching a large trout on a dry fly.

bright fly designed to annoy them into striking. These fish are absolutely enormous. I caught the biggest trout of the trip on the Tauranga. An entry in my journal from that day reads:

"April 23rd, Lake Taupo. The biggest fish of the day was eight pounds. He went half way into my backing and around a corner. I thought I might lose him. It turned out to be a beautiful hen. None of the trout we caught were much less than seven pounds, and their colors were absolutely incredible. Their bodies darken up, and the red turns fiery along the side, especially in their face that lights up with fire. The big one I caught was fresh from the lake, and still very silvery, but she had that seductive red head."

There are also helicopter fly-outs to the backcountry, where you find more conventional rainbow trout fishing. Here you are unlikely to spend very much time fishing the rocky runs where the brown trout might be. You will be moving straight from pool to pool, where you can watch the dozens of large rainbows swimming away in absolutely crystal-clear water. You fish to them as you would normally fish to a rainbow.

LEFT: *Here a guide lands a spawning rainbow from the Taurangi-Taupo River. This river drains directly into Lake Taupo, the county's largest lake. Although the lake is not salt water, these fish behave exactly like steelheads coming into the rivers to spawn from the sea. The original stock of rainbows that came to the North Island from California is believed to have been steelheads.*

BELOW: *This was the largest trout we caught on the whole trip. I hooked this beautiful eight-and-a-half-pound hen on the Taurangi-Taupo River. She was coming upstream from Lake Taupo to spawn, and snapped at an egg pattern like a heavy salmon. Then she turned and made a powerful run straight downstream, and almost got away.*

ABOVE: *When casting to a single large brown, it is a good idea to use long casts so the fish doesn't see you or hear your feet crunching on the rocks. Here, on the Crow River, South Island, a roll cast is a good way to get all of that line off the water and start over. The fish rarely take on the first presentation.*

The real joy here is that rainbows are much more acrobatic than the other trout. Seeing them come up out of water is a sight to remember. And there is another major attraction. High above the lake is the recently active volcano, a constant reminder that you are on the Pacific Rim. It felt as though a local Maori god was watching our every cast.

TACKLE AND GEAR

ROD AND REEL

The fishing you will be doing here may be much more varied than it was in the South Island, and you may well need a wider range of gear. Firstly, you will certainly want your basic 5-weight trout rod. You will use this in the mountains when you fly out in the helicopter. Despite the fact that the streams in the backcountry are not particularly large – in fact some of them are quite small – they still carry very large trout. You will also want to bring a heavier 7-weight rod to cast Glo-bugs across long distances or in heavy water conditions. Some of the rivers flowing into Lake Taupo can be enormous, especially with any rain, and you will need some heavier casting power.

Finally, if you are going to try for one of the really large fish in the lakes, you will want to take a much heavier 9–10 weight rod. This will be appropriate to cast high-density, fast-sinking line, or shooting heads far from the boat to strip a large streamer through the water at depth.

Make sure if you are going to do this that you have a reel that holds a fair bit of backing. Although you probably won't need it, these steelhead-like rainbows can get their mind set on going up a river. They will run quite hard, especially in the open water, and if you interrupt their thought process with a hook in their mouth, they get very angry. Your drag and your backing will help you save what may be, with some luck, a record fish.

LINES AND LEADERS

For the mountain fishing, you will not want much more than a 9-foot leader with 3-4x tippet material. The rainbows did not seem particularly hard to convince. They were certainly much easier than the brown trout. You can stick with the lighter tippet if you want, but remember these fish get big, and they are incredibly acrobatic. The weight forward line to match your rod will be perfectly sufficient to fish these pools.

If you are going to be fishing the estuaries at the mouths of the big rivers, you will need some more substantial lines. A high-density, fast-sinking line to get down to the large females is a must. The faster it sinks, the better, as rainbows will rest at considerable depths, depending on the water temperatures.

Finally, you will want to get either a floating line with a sinking tip, or an intermediate line. This will enable you to get your flies to fish at less severe depths. Depending on the day, many of them will be circulating just beneath the surface. Don't forget to allow yourself plenty of backing. In most cases, you will not need it, but this is where you will find the biggest fish of your life. You don't want to lose it by running out of line.

THE FLY BOX

Depending on the time of year you come, you will probably want to try catching the spawning rainbows. These fish do not take readily to a typical trout fly. Over here, they use Glo-bugs. This is essentially a stimulator. It is a number 4–8 hook with a lot of fluorescent yarn tied on like a crab. Some weighted eyes to help it

sink and look somewhat realistic will also help. In this vein, some egg patterns also work, as trout like to eat their own species' eggs.

In the mountains, the typical trout flies will work. Dry flies and nymphs are universal, and the usual American and English patterns will work.

Rainbows on the North Island are much more likely to take wet streamer flies than the brown trout on the South Island. This is also the only way you can catch the large fish in the lakes and stream mouths. The Muddler Minnow will be very effective, as will the Clouser Minnow, and a bead-headed Marabou Streamer. Aside from this, always ask the locals, as they fish a great deal here.

ESSENTIAL KIT

Chest waders will be very helpful when fishing the Tongariro. When we were there, the river was absolutely enormous, and gushing tremendously. The waders saved me. Many rivers up in the mountains will be easily worked with just hip waders, but ask your guide before going.

Polarized sunglasses will be important here as well. Although spotting trout holding in feeding lanes is not the name of the game here, there are still a great many fish to be seen in this "gin-clear" water.

Aside from that, bug spray will help with the midges. A net will help you with the big monsters, and bring a camera so your friends don't accuse you of telling fishy tales when you get home.

CONSERVATION WATCH

New Zealand is another country renowned for its pristine surroundings. The success of the trout species introduced into New Zealand has been due in large part to the cooperation of the locals, and of the tourists who come to fish these waters, but New Zealand's fresh-water trout fisheries are well managed by the fish and game council. Catch-and-release practices, as well as management of the riverbanks, have combined to make this one of the most successful acclimatization efforts anywhere in the world.

However, these efforts are not without their problems. Many fisherman still fail to observe bag limits or restrictions. This over-fishing can seriously damage the size and genetic makeup of the fish in any stretch of water. If undersized fish are constantly taken from a river, existing generations will be unable to reproduce, and fish numbers could well suffer the consequences. Low fish numbers would put more emphasis on restocking, and the efforts being put into addressing other serious environmental problems will be reduced.

PREVIOUS PAGE: *Farmlands near Turangi on the North Island. The countryside in New Zealand is a vast array of mountains, coastline, wetlands, farmlands, and prairies. For such a small country, the natives have access to the best of everything.*

BELOW: *Although trout are not native to New Zealand, an old fishing culture followed the fish when they arrived. Although these reels may not work so well anymore, these timeless fly patterns certainly will. Among them are the Royal Wulff, the Pheasant Tail Nymph, the Hare's Ear Nymph, the Parachute Adams, a large caddis, a spun deer hair popper, and other variations.*

Lead poisoning of wildlife has been a problem in rivers. Some studies have shown that as much as 14 per cent of waterfowl are killed every year by lead shot and split shot left in the water. In Britain, lead fishing sinkers weighing less than 28g have been outlawed since 1987. The reason for this is that when a bird accidentally ingests the lead while feeding, the acidity in the bird's stomach and digestive tract causes toxic lead salts to be released into the body. Depending on the amount of lead, a bird will die anywhere between two days to three weeks later. One study in the Waikato Fish and Game District found that 13.9 per cent of mallards had ingested lead shot, and were severely poisoned. Hopefully, this disturbing revelation will open some people's eyes, and fishermen and hunters alike will move to steel, bismuth, or tungsten as an alternative to lead.

ABOVE: *David Pike, here fishing on the Motueka River, South Island, was the best guide I have ever had anywhere in the world. He has eagle eyes and can pick out a fish in the river in even the most difficult places.*

Mick Mason at the Motueka Lodge can put you in touch, and if you can arrange a trip with him, you'll never have a better fishing experience.

To learn more about wildlife conservation, contact:
The Royal Forest and Bird Protection Society
PO Box 631
Wellington, New Zealand
Tel: 04 385-7374

THE FOUNTAIN
BHUTAN

PARO RIVER, BHUTAN

It doesn't matter what some people tell you, or what garbled nonsense certain philosophers would have us all believe; life on Earth is a glorious thing. The worst of these moralizers tell us that life is an endless struggle against adversity, that what doesn't kill us makes us stronger, and survival in itself is what we should hope for, because, in this world of so much pain and misery, the forces acting against us will never let up and never cease. This is a powerful appeal to our fears, especially when put in the hypnotic prose of learned philosophers such as Nietzsche. Yet the defeat of these arguments lies in what they lack. They ignore the glorious in ourselves and in the world around us. They ignore the very meaning of life.

LEFT: *Fly fishing on the Mo River, Punakha.*

Inextricably bound to human nature is the desire for that which is great – for the things out on the horizon that will endlessly fuel our desire to sail to them. Christopher Columbus once wrote in his ship's log that "...the sea will bring each man new hope, as sleep brings dreams." Beyond every horizon, there is a new land, and upon every sea, a new adventure. If a man knew with absolute certainty that there was nothing over the horizon, and that the ocean would be forever calm, he would not set sail upon it unless he had lost all hope and his days were done. And it is this hope that coats the heart of fly-fishers with gold.

Some people find us foolish; others think we are just crazy. Either way, those who do not fish cannot possibly understand why we are so religiously devoted to what we do. Deep in the heart of every devoted fly-fisherman is a yearning, a thirst for the absolute best in life, and an anchor set firmly in the sea of hope.

BELOW: *On top of the world. Nothing could be better than fly-fishing on the roof of the Himalayan mountains. Bhutan has a vast array of excellent trout rivers, and a healthy ecosystem to support them. Here, I'm trying to figure out what language the trout in Bhutan speak.*

Hope is one of our oldest and deepest feelings – that intruder that takes control of us, paints great expectations on our face, and a childlike excitement on our hearts. Our first encounters with hope came during childhood when we a saw a puppy for sale through a forbidding window, or an out-of-reach pellet gun in a sports store, like a cookie on a far away shelf. At that single moment, there wasn't a thing in the world we wouldn't willingly have given up just for the simple thrill of holding that little piece of Nirvana in our hands. Being carried out of the store was enough to break your heart, as you watched your object of desire sail away like a doomed ship carrying your lover from shore.

The object of a fly-fisherman's yearning is to be sought on the river. Our prayers find an echo in the dark. We learn that there is always that little piece of perfection to be had somewhere in the churning water, and its lure is as strong as love itself. We are constantly reaching into the aquatic world in search of all the little pieces that together make us whole. An angler's life is the story of an endless quest for perfection. Never will we catch the greatest fish in the river and be able to say, "*enough*." Because there is always more out there; there are bigger fish, and the river is constantly changing. But one thing remains the same; the search for the ultimate catch – the Big One. It is out there, but it is more myth than reality. The Big One is a concept that we have formed in our minds to help explain what we are hunting for in the foggiest reaches of the river.

Those of us who find beauty in fish are fascinated by every catch we make. Somewhere in the tangles of our mind we believe that all the beauty that we discover within the river must come from some wondrous source. There must be a supreme creator of all of the beautiful things we see. To some, this great source is the Christian God, while to the Buddhists, what we see has been here for all eternity, but there are those of us who believe that somewhere in the river of life, each catch we make will reveal to us a tiny piece of that great whole. And, some day, if we can fit together enough of these tiny pieces, we just might get an idea of what that perfect whole looks like. Yet, we must never forget that each fish we catch was there long before we found it, and the egg from which it was born was only part of an endless life cycle stretching back all the way to the beginning, when all of the world was submerged in water. As the mountains pushed their way through the surface, the world's creatures were there to climb them. And in the rivers that still stream down their sides, we find fish constantly pushing upward through the current to seek the fountainhead from which their world began.

In the evenings, as we stand by the river's edge and watch this endless procession marching by, we never fail to make that one last cast in the hope of hooking the perfect fish. My hook is always on the water, seeking more pieces of the whole, ready for it to strike from underneath.

In my life, there has been pain and glory, heartache, and happiness. But, most importantly, I've known love; and if it hasn't brought me to the place I seek, it certainly points me in the right direction – it is Gatsby's green light flashing in the darkness. Through it all, once we have found the light, there is nothing that will keep us from returning to fish in the twilight of another day.

The following is an excerpt from my journal on May 2nd, 1998 from Bhutan: "…I seriously could not believe what was happening. It almost looked like they were spawning. Huge fish were leaping right out of the water in the lee of a large rock. I saw mayflies, and I tried nymphs and dries. I knew they could see them because they were jumping all around them. They just wouldn't take. It made me think a lot about my piece on hope. I was talking to myself. I was kissing each new fly. I was almost hysterical watching them jump. I would have done anything to have caught one of those big ones. But life goes on and my dreams will be filled with the wild rush of that night. In dreams, Alex swims with the fishes."

A BRIEF HISTORY

Bhutan, which literally means "*Sleeping Dragon*," is an ancient kingdom, complete with legends and mysteries. It is a small Buddhist country, nestled high in the Himalayan Mountains. The people are proud of the fact that they are the only country remaining in the area that has never been conquered by an outside power. For centuries, few people outside the Buddhist world ever visited this small area of lush Himalayan countryside. Relations with neighboring India are strong, but there is very little commercial industry to necessitate many visitors. Furthermore, to protect the country's ancient culture, the royal family greatly limited the number of tourist visas issued until recently.

When you visit Bhutan, you will be amazed at the beauty of this land. You will see enormous monasteries built dramatically into the sides of jagged mountains. Hydrangeas and other flowers grow scattered throughout the valleys. Worshippers show their devotion by walking hundreds of miles without food, praying as they go. Outsiders receive friendly waves, as they are still a rare sight in this tiny kingdom. A visitor waking up in this country that time has forgotten might think he or she had stumbled upon heaven. And to add to its paradise-like qualities, tucked far away from the rest of civilization, Bhutan proves to be one of the world's least known fly-fishing treasures.

Bhutan has only recently become a new branch on the fast-growing tree of fly-fishing. It has blossomed, in a sense, by royal decree. The late King Jigme Dorji Wangchuk introduced the fish in 1954. The trout ova were brought in from Kashmir, India (and hence from the English stock) in closed, refrigerated trucks.

PREVIOUS PAGE: The Punakha Valley is one of the most beautiful places in Bhutan, and there is a glorious freestone river beneath it that holds trout. Many of the houses overlooking the valley are built in the typical oriental style that one can see throughout the country.

They were introduced through temporary hatcheries into the western valleys of Haa, Thimphu, and Paro. His Royal Highness, the King, watched the success of these fishy pioneers closely. After several years, it was concluded that these first brown trout had successfully settled into the rivers, and were ready to be introduced permanently throughout Bhutan.

Their offspring were taken to the valleys of the east, including Punakha, Bumthang, and Nikkachu. Some rainbow trout were placed in the high valleys and spring waters of Gangtey and Gagona, and some experimental stocks were even placed in several high mountain lakes between 13,000 and 15,000 feet. The fish were then left to fend for themselves without any supporting hatchery programs, and there is now an especially strong mix of rainbow and brown trout in a variety of rivers between the altitudes of 4,500 and 11,000 feet. When the king died, his brother, HRH Prince Namgyel Wangchuck continued his work. The Prince, who

ABOVE: *The ancient Tachogang monastery, or chorten, beside the Paro River. In Bhutan, religion is everywhere. Near almost every river we fished, there was an old chorten like this one. They are holy places, each with a different meaning for the Buddhists.*

ABOVE: *This brown trout caught in the Mo River was feeding right along the side of the bank when we arrived. If our guide Ugyen hadn't spotted him immediately, we might have spooked him. Instead, Ugyen caught him on a dry fly and released him unharmed.*

is the uncle to the present-day king, is one of the great personalities in the kingdom of Bhutan. It is said that he speaks around 16 different language dialects. No one has trekked the length and breadth of the country in the way that the Prince has. He works with his people as a social worker, and is also a knowledgeable outdoorsman. He is also, we are happy to say, a keen fly-fisherman.

The trout have been living there now, on their own in a country that is new to them, since their first introduction. Rainbows and brown trout seem to dominate in different rivers. And like all the great trout destinations, I am still haunted today by thoughts of the fish swimming there.

THE BHUTAN EXPERIENCE

By any stretch of the imagination, Bhutan is one of the best trout fisheries in the world. The quantity of the rivers is such that you can find a great variety in the character of the rivers. Most are classic freestone streams – both large and small. Yet, when we arrived in the sprawling Gangtey valley, we fished a spectacular river just like a chalk stream.

Because of this variety and the available space, we moved locations every couple of days for the two weeks we were in Bhutan. Our fishing felt like one grand exploration. The country is very rural, and there are no access rights, no fly-shops. You just pick your favorite stretch of the river and fish. Almost everywhere you go will produce sizeable fish.

As I mentioned before, the country is very small, and there are few fly-fishermen there. Your arrival in any given town is greeted with excitement, because not only are you an outsider, but you also have some very odd looking equipment, and you appear to be doing something very strange down by the river. (A local's idea of fishing is getting a dough ball and a hook, and waiting.) So, don't be surprised if you find a small group of kids trailing along behind you.

Besides the thrill of feeling like a true fly-fishing pioneer, you can confidently expect an incredible all-around experience. There is only one guide there, Ugyen Rinzin, and he does a superb job of making sure you have a great time. He has his own wooden lodge way out in the far eastern end of the country. He knows dozens of people with guesthouses and lodges in between there and Paro. In addition, he used to be a page in the royal court, and also knows His Royal Highness, the Prince, quite well. This enabled us to have privileged access to a number of different rivers.

In addition to the excellent rainbow and brown trout fishing, there are other game fish as well. The most notable amongst these is the golden mahseer. The fish comes from some old fisherman's dreams, reaching sizes in excess of 100 pounds. They can be found at altitudes of less than 4,000 feet. Preferring warmer climates with water cascading down quickly from higher elevations, they are only found in the southern regions of the country.

When we were there, increasing concern over the pressure on the golden mahseer had led to a ban on all mahseer fishing. The Department of Forests is responsible for conservation and anti-poaching measures. But as 72 per cent of the country is covered in forests, and has animals ranging from trout and mahseer to eagles and Bengal tigers, their job can be quite overwhelming. Hopefully, a proper conservation program of catch and release will reintroduce angling for mahseer in the near future. In the meantime, the trout were quite enough for me.

TACKLE AND GEAR
RODS AND REELS

For the trout fishing, you will want to bring equipment for a number of different fishing scenarios. We fished freestone rivers, both large and small, and one slow chalk stream. The force and level of the water also varied a good deal.

You must bring a good 5-weight. It is the perfect size rod for the slow but wide chalk stream in the Gangtey Valley. Some of the fish in there are five to six pounds, so you don't want to go too light. A 5-weight is also ideal for the smaller and medium-sized freestone rivers you will fish. In the bigger rivers, I used an 8-weight, but I could have gone even heavier. The heavier rod will help not only with the distance you want, but also with the heavy winds that sweep across the top of the world. With some of the rivers being as forceful as they are, it is important to remember that you may want to use heavily weighted lines and flies to get deep, and this adds to the case for using bigger rods on a couple of the rivers.

Aside from that advice, always rely on your preferences. A 3-weight rod will not get in the way, and it could be fun on some of the smaller streams.

LINES AND LEADERS

The fishing was not overly technical. A double-tapered line, while nice for line control, is not necessary. Bring a weight-forward floating line for almost every situation. This will be the best all-purpose line you can bring.

For the heavier rivers, you will need a fast-sinking line capable of bringing a heavy fly or streamer down low. Some of the rivers up there can really roar when the water is up. Without a fast-sinking line, or at least a floating line with a 30 foot sinking tip, the tension and speed of the water will keep your line too near the surface. The fish may be down low.

5x tippet will be the best all-around tippet to finish off a 9–12 foot leader in most smaller rivers. For the larger ones, you will need some 0x or 2x leaders to turn over the heavier flies at long distances.

THE FLY BOX

Try to bring a full array of trout flies, both wet and dry. In the spring, there will be a great many dry flies coming off the water. I saw a number of small mayflies and caddis hatching.

The Dad's Favorite is the name of a New Zealand dry fly that worked well here. It is a small brown mayfly with a very slender body tied with the quills from a duck wing, so its texture looks very realistic; it has a brown wing and hackle. Bring a lot of size 12–16 dry flies like these. Also, bring their accompanying nymphs. Use bead heads if all else fails. These fish are not pressured very much at all, so when they see the flash of the bead, they will take!

For the heavier rivers, use your sinking line with some big heavy flies. Marabou streamers and Wooly Buggers always work, no matter where you are. Just make sure they have got some lead in the body, or a bead head to help them get down in the deeper parts.

PREVIOUS PAGE: *The rivers in Bhutan are classic freestone rivers. Many of them have gigantic boulders which provide excellent pocket fishing. Crossing some of the rivers on a Bhutanese suspension bridge, like this one over the Paro River, can be a test of a man's stability. Some of the rickety bridges are hundreds of feet above the water.*

LEFT: *Here, Ugyen Rinzen, the only fly-fishing outfitter in Bhutan, casts in the Mo River, one of the best trout rivers in the country. Ugyen used to run a fly manufacturing company that would export its flies internationally. There are not many fly-fisherman in Bhutan, and Ugyen is only one of a handful who knows where to go. The prince of Bhutan is also an avid fly-fisherman and travels from border to border with his rod and reel.*

PREVIOUS PAGE: *This quaint village in the Gangtey Valley held some great memories for us on the trip. We fished a beautiful chalk stream and caught dozens of fish. At night, we danced with the local girls, and stayed up late talking by candlelight. The farmers had problems with wild boar and had to stay up all night in shifts walking through their fields singing with bells.*

BELOW: *This small shop is in the town of Khasadrapchu. The locals don't see very many tourists in Bhutan and treat you just like anyone else. Outside many of these shops is a tin burning with a stick of incense. There is also quite often a picture of King Jigme Singye Wangchuck.*

I also saw some very large stone fly shedding on the rocks. Bring a few large, weighted stone fly nymphs, and check the bottom of rocks in shallow water. If Ugyen is your guide, he will have plenty of flies. His first business in Bhutan made flies for export. He wanted to see how they behaved in the water, and one day a fish took! That was it. They still manufacture them, so even though you will not find the kinds of stores that sell rods and reels, you can find some flies.

ESSENTIAL KIT

Bring a good camera. The things you see won't be found anywhere else in the world. There are huge Buddhist monasteries built into the mountainside, incredible rivers, interesting people – you will definitely want a camera.

You will also want warm waders. The water here comes straight from the top of the world, so it is extremely cold. Some of the rivers are also quite powerful and difficult to wade, so make sure you have a wading belt in case you fall.

Even though you are up in the mountains, the sun is incredibly strong, and sunblock is important. You can get burned quickly because the atmosphere up there is thin. Be careful.

As a precaution, bring something for an upset stomach. You are in a foreign culture eating different food. Everything we had prepared for us was gourmet quality; but one day I bought some meat pie from a street vendor. I will just say that it did not sit well for a day or two. If this happens to you, make sure you are ready. I was not.

CONSERVATION WATCH

Bhutan is lucky in some respects to be so isolated from the outside world. The country enjoys 72 per cent forest coverage. Almost every mountain and glen is covered in lush trees and flowers. The country also has very little industrial production, so the pollution levels are quite low. There are cars, but not very many of them. The air is clear, and it is heaven for the trout. But nonetheless, as in all countries, there are some conservation problems.

Having so few fly-fishermen is a mixed blessing. While the fish may not see a fly too often, there are very few of the conservation measures that usually accompany the fly-fishing culture.

With an abundance of good trout in the river, the locals see this as a great opportunity for food and a commercial livelihood. On many of the rivers we saw rudimentary fishing dams that trap fish. The poacher will then net the trapped pool, and sell the fish. It is actually considered poaching, as there is a limit on the number of fish you are allowed to keep, but it happens, nonetheless.

The National Conservation Section, headed by Dr Sangay Wangchuk, a Yale graduate, is a government office in charge of all conservation in the country. While there is considerable concern about this pressure on the trout, enforcing the laws in such a rural country is very difficult, especially with limited personnel.

Trash and garbage overflow from urban areas is always a problem. While there is very little that can be done about it, Dr Wangchuk has made great strides in raising the awareness of the local population. There has recently been a total ban on all plastic bags in the country, and this has helped the problem.

Yet, despite these problems, Bhutan still enjoys a thriving and diverse ecosystem. Due to the extraordinary variety of flora and fauna that flourish at various altitudes, Bhutan has been recognized by the World Wildlife Fund as one of the world's few Biodiversity Hotspots.

If you are interested in getting involved or learning more about the natural habitats of Bhutan, including the fishing sanctuaries there, you can contact:

Dr Sangay Wangchuk
National Conservation Section
Ministry of Agriculture
Thimphu, Kingdom of Bhutan
Tel: (975) 2 – 325042
Fax: (975) 2 – 325475

Royal Society for the Protection of Nature
Dr Kinley Dorjee – Executive Director
Thimphu, Kingdom of Bhutan
(ph) (975) 2 – 322056
(fax) (975) 2 – 323189

World Wildlife Federation
Dr Kinley Dorjee – Local Representative
Thimphu, Kingdom of Bhutan
(ph) (975) 2 – 323528
(fax) (975) 2 – 323518

FISHING FOR THE MOON
BY SALMON LIGHT
IRELAND

DROWES FISHERY, KENLOUGH, IRELAND

They told me before I arrived in Ireland that it takes a thousand casts to catch an Atlantic salmon. A thousand and one casts later I had something to smile about, having single-handedly disproven an age-old theory that had been believed by countless fly-fishermen before me.

The conditions this year have worked against us, but with the enthusiasm I gained through my ground-breaking discovery, I set out on my own to catch this elusive fish for the first time. I soaked up all the information I could to develop my own secret tactic to pursue the Atlantic Salmon. Our local friend in the fisheries office in Laureen Park told me that the best thing to do would be to visit the Wellington Pub and down three pints of Guinness!

LEFT: *Erriff River, Delphi.*

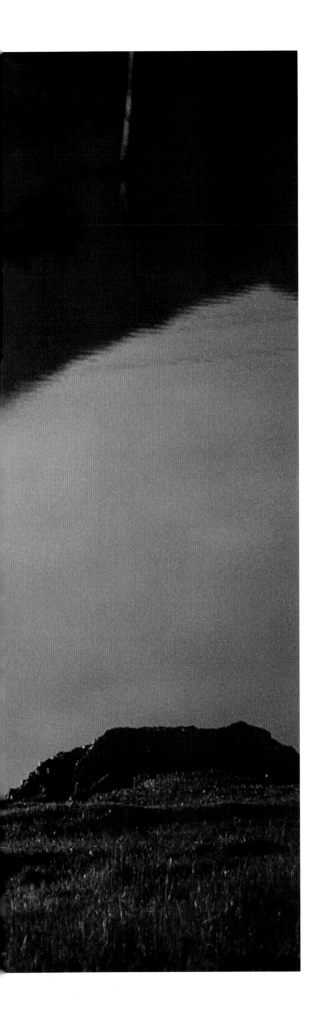

"Interesting advice," I thought. Our previous ghillie had said that only five pints would be sufficient. In fact, I heard this advice so often that I began to think I might start finding flies tied from barley and hops in the local fly shops. They say that God invented alcohol to keep the Irish from ruling the world. What it didn't keep them from doing was spending their time fly-fishing. So, I figured there must be some merit to what they said. After all, fly-fishing seems to be a way of life amongst many of the locals here; they even put a salmon on their 20 pence coins.

So, while we ate dinner at night, we would fill our stomachs with Guinness hoping to find enlightenment and discover what we could possibly do to make this leg of the trip a success. I don't know what state of mind we reached, but it sure wasn't enlightenment. My mind turned to mush, and I came up with a theory contrary to the beliefs of everyone in the area who knew anything about fishing.

High tide that night would be sometime during the middle of the night. The high water should, I reckoned, make it easier for the salmon to make it to their spawning grounds, and I was determined to be there when they made their push. So, I set my alarm for 3.00 a.m. to be down at the estuary on time.

When my alarm went off in the wee hours of the night, my head was bulging and sore and felt like a wobbly balloon filled to the breaking point with Guinness. I shook off any yearnings to return to bed and quietly snuck out of the house into the cold air of an Irish morning. When I first got into the car, I must have thought I was back in the States because I got pulled over for driving on the right-hand side of the road. Luckily, the policeman was a fly-fisherman, and he was quick to tell me that, "Ya cahnt cahtch the salmon in the mid'l o' the night." But he let me go and try anyway. Somewhere in the back of my mind, I was tempted to believe what he said, but something was pulling me down to the sea that night.

I parked the Land Rover on the bridge and used the light on the rear door to rig my gear. My eyes hadn't quite adjusted yet, but the conditions looked good. The stream dropped from pool to pool as it rushed into the sea 200 yards away in the darkness. There was a thin silvery line of waves illuminated by the moon that gently washed up the shore every few seconds.

Walking down to the water, I felt out of my element in this strange country. Peering over the stone walls, it was just me and the secrets of the night. Along the water there was just one abandoned stone house, and silhouetted on the ridge in the distance was an old stone castle – equally dark and haunting. The pub down the street was empty and the echoes of the last drunks had long since died away.

LEFT: *Reflections. A day of fishing can find a fisherman lost deeply in thoughts. Here, beside Lough Inagh, near Ballynahinch, with the mountains looming on the far bank, it is hard not to reflect on the beauty of the Irish countryside. Lush grass, large rocks, mountains, and endless rivers and lakes to fish make this an angler's heaven.*

I paid out some line and started to do some casting. Normally, fishing for Atlantic salmon can be very exhausting, not only on the body, but also on the mind. But doing it in the middle of the night, when everyone I had spoken to had been emphatic that it was the worst time to fish, was downright depressing. However, I thought that something must be there.

If nothing else, it was a beautiful night. There was a star-filled sky, as broad and vast as it had ever been. It's usually rainy or cloudy in this part of the world, so the stars were a rare treat. And directly above me was a huge yellow moon. It was that same luxurious harvest moon that I had found following me periodically ever since I was a child, and it brought back smiles and memories of other moonlit nights. Funny that a cold rock thousands of miles away could make one feel at home. I looked back into the water and saw its wavy reflection at the head of the pool. As it moved across the sky, its reflection edged its way up the current. The hours passed by, and I watched the moon's warm glow inch its way up the river and even threaten to disappear under the dark bridge.

So I began to pass the time by casting my fly right into the moonshine. I threw my line time after time as if to hook the moon and hold it back, briefly, before it made its big push and disappeared up the river. Sometimes I'd miss and splash the reflection into a hundred little droplets of moonlight. But sometimes, I'd send it just right and lay the fly on top of the moon if only a brief moment before it hit the water. If I blinked at just the right second, I'd be left with a picture in

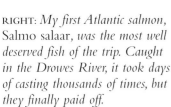

RIGHT: *My first Atlantic salmon,* Salmo salaar, *was the most well deserved fish of the trip. Caught in the Drowes River, it took days of casting thousands of times, but they finally paid off.*

An Atlantic salmon is one of the most difficult fish in the world to catch, but when you bring one in, nothing could be more beautiful. They are shiny silver, many times with a hint of blue running down their back. Fresh in form the cold, dark waters of the North Atlantic, it is a pure glimpse of the perfect fish.

my mind of the silhouette of a salmon fly sitting on top of the moon as if on a moonlit silver platter. It made me believe the stories that Christ and his disciples were all fishermen, because only God could come up with an image this beautiful.

But, as I spent more time looking into this beautiful void, I began to notice something peculiar. The flashes of light that I had thought were patches of moon were not all moving in the exact same direction, and some didn't disappear. It took an hour or two for my eyes to adjust but, once they had, I could see what was happening. Beneath the surface of the water, the moonlight continued on down into the darkness, illuminating an entire world of sub-aquatic magic. A salmon run was under way, and I was watching them as they got caught in the moonbeams for just a fleeting moment. There were discreet little flashes of light, filtered by the water on its seaward journey.

At first, they actually looked more like patches of moon being reflected in the ripples. Yet, you can't mistake the sight of a salmon, any more than you can miss the sound of a secret. Beneath me, just feet away, and in all but another world, was one of the Earth's greatest phenomena underway. Before long, our worlds began to

ABOVE: *Finlough – this lake in front of the Delphi Lodge in Ireland was full of salmon, and these sea trout, Salmo trutta. Many people find the sea trout as much fun to catch as the salmon. Unfortunately, disease and commercial fisheries are ruining the sea trout populations, but there is now a large movement underway to save them. It is called S.O.S. – Save Our Sea trout.*

meet, as I heard some of the larger ones breaking through the surface as they leaped up the white water falls just beneath me.

I'd been casting furiously, but not accurately, as I was too busy trying to see through the water and get a glimpse of the whole fish. My mind was full of disbelief and an intoxicating midnight wonder. The moment had come upon me too fast. I've seen salmon move before, but never in a collected push like this, and never framed in the world with so many odd factors coming together at the same time to produce a sight so beautiful. I began to realize that the fly was not going to interest them. But, it didn't matter. I could picture it floating by them like a

BELOW: *Dapping is one of the oldest forms of angling in Ireland. The hatches here, on Lough Corrib, are famous for their two- to three-inch mayflies. Anglers here tie a large mayfly onto their line and let it dance in the wind over the surface of the water as if the fly were actually laying eggs. Trout will leap into the air to catch them.*

sparkling Christmas ornament suspended in the darkness before a child. When pulled by the current, it would shoot by them like a star. I looked back to the sky and marveled at what an intimate connection there was between the salmon and the moon on this unforgettable evening; how the wonders of the world could be summed up in this bold river.

Far away in time, when it all began, the universe exploded out in the darkness. All the stars and all the elements in existence were sent flying out into space to begin their cycle. Even to this day, galaxies are constantly being formed as stars explode and contract again.

The cycle of life is happening everywhere. Even in this river, which lifted itself out of the ocean millennia ago, the cycle continues. Every salmon I could see beneath me had once left this very river. We were younger then, and so were they. When only the size of a twig, they had turned their backs to the mountain, and made a dash for the open sea. There they exploded in all directions, and swam into the depths where we could never go. These tiny fish, who can move up to fifty miles a day, will swim thousands of miles during their lives. They'll learn to flee from the sharks, to jump from the whales, and to compete with each other. They'll follow their older and wiser relatives and learn how to grow up. Then, at some point, a grand force will pull them back to where it all began.

They will turn around and bee-line it straight back to the mouth of the river in which they were born. And, at high tide, their blood boiling, they will enter the river, full of purpose and determination. They will have made a decision not to eat for another year until they find their way up the mountain, to the very same place that they once emerged from their small eggs.

That night, as I stood beneath the moon, they swam away beneath me. The moon crept its way up the river and up the mountain, and so did they. Like a river of stars accelerating its way back to the giant epicenter of existence, each one of these fish carried with it the seeds of the next explosion.

From a little packet of eggs, so small and translucent as to be invisible, the future salmon float with the potential of another galaxy. When the water's gentle hand pulls them open, they will ignite, and the river will once again be full of stars pouring into the open sea. Some day the moon will return to catch it all again, and someone like me will be standing by the water's edge. Maybe that person will be thinking about their past, or their future, or someone they miss, but if they look a little harder into the dark waters they will see the same glimmers of light. And if they know what it is, they will know that life is pouring out into the dark oceans that seem so vast. Somewhere out on the horizon, where whales meet and salmon are learning to grow, two small fish in the sea will find each other under the same moonlit night, and marvel that life is so beautiful.

A BRIEF HISTORY

As in Scotland, trying to find the origins of angling in Ireland is like trying to discover the origins of literature. One could spend a lifetime tracing back the stories, the tales of salmon and fishing, and days spent angling in the beautiful Irish countryside.

However, we do know that fishing for trout and salmon was well under way in Britain and the surrounding isles by the early 1400s. Thanks to the 15th-century *Treatyse on Fysshynge Wyth an Angle* by Dame Juliana Berners, we know that English-speaking tribes were well versed in the fishing tradition. Yet we know that the Irish were taking an interest in the comings and goings of the salmon long before this time. Being one of the most mysterious fish in the world, it is hard to imagine that anyone could look at these large silver creatures as they leap through the water and fail to become engaged in the mystery of their cyclical nature, linked as they are to the seasons of the year.

Every spring the fish returns to begin its annual migration upstream into the walled corridors of the beginnings of life. The mysteries are endless. It's a wonderful feeling to look out at a cold winter's morning over the Atlantic and marvel that somewhere out on the shadowy horizons thousands of these fish are growing and feeding in the darkest and deepest waters on the planet. They can travel to places that men would become legendary for reaching. Even the most primitive man must have realized that these fish were coming from the ocean into the rivers every year.

Upon their return, the salmon bring the deepness and darkness of the oceans with them. It is almost frightening to stand near a run of salmon fresh in from the ocean. As they leap and push upward past the mountain, you squint your eyes in an effort to see deeper into their souls, to crystallize their image. What have they seen in the past nine months? Where have they been? Has theirs been an experience more terrifying than a nightmare or more beautiful than a song? And, most importantly, what keeps them coming back year after year? What's on their mind?

I cannot discover when in time man first caught a salmon in Irish waters, but I do know that all the way back to the beginning of *Homo sapiens*, man has been kneeling by the river and marveling over the same mysteries that I have always wondered about. Many cultures recorded these primitive beginnings in song, many wrote stories or painted pictures on a rock wall. This being Ireland, the people expressed themselves in poetry. In fact, poets and salmon are what much of Irish culture is all about.

The earliest poem that I have been able to find that reflects man's obsession with watching the salmon was written in pagan times by Amergin. Amergin can lay claim to being Ireland's first poet – a distinguished title considering that some

PREVIOUS PAGE: *Spey casting on the Ballynahinch River, in Ireland. Spey casting was certainly named for the Spey River in Scotland, but the Irish also use double-handed spey casting rods. It is an efficient way to quickly throw up to 100 feet of line in one sweeping motion. As fishing for salmon can take "1000 casts," it is important to save your energy.*

LEFT: *Here, the Drowes River empties into the North Atlantic near Bundoran. When the tides rise and cover these rocks, the salmon make mad runs to swim as far up the river as possible while the water is high. In view of the distant castle, this is where I caught my first salmon.*

of his intellectual descendants include the likes of James Joyce and William Yeats. Amergin was brother to Evir, Ir, and Eremon, the first Milesian princes who colonized Ireland many centuries before the birth of Christ. The following is his poem, widely considered to be Ireland's first:

THE MYSTERY

I am the wind which breathes upon the sea,
I am the wave of the ocean,
I am the murmur of the billows,
I am the ox of the seven combats,
I am the vulture upon the rocks,
I am a beam of the sun,
I am the fairest of plants,
I am a wild boar in valour,
I am a salmon in the water,
I am a lake in the plain,
I am a word of science,
I am the point of the lance in battle,
I am the God who created in the head the fire.
Who is it who throws light into the meeting on the mountain?
Who announces the ages of the moon?
Who teaches the place where couches the sun?
        (If not I?)

This metaphysical plunge into the elements of nature and the borders between reality and the supernatural is one that lifts the soul to a point of breathlessness. *"The wave of the ocean… a beam of the sun… the point of the lance in battle…"* These are all elements in life that have a tremendous gravity in their expression. They are the basic elements of the natural world that make us ponder the existence of a higher power, a power that is capable of the creation of such things, *"I am a salmon in the water."* There is no doubt that when the first salmon was spotted in Irish waters, it was a cause for amazement and wonder. Only such a feeling could evoke such words of importance from anyone, whether it be a warrior or a poet, or both, as is the case with Amergin.

It is impossible to know for sure through the mention of salmon in this early poem whether or not the first inhabitants of Ireland actually caught salmon for sport. But what we can deduce is that the spirit behind fly-fishing had been born. A mystery and love for this beautiful animal had captured the author's heart, much as it has captured centuries worth of English speaking anglers. This is the essence

of fly-fishing. As any good fisherman knows, a nice day on the river is possible without taking a single fish. Some people take enjoyment from seeing ducks and herons and other wildlife. Others like to be near water, while still others like the peace and tranquility of the outdoors. But just as surely as I stand by a misty stretch of water, Amergin sat by a cool salmon stream and was overcome by a tremendous rush of excitement.

In today's busy world it is sometimes difficult to find a place where you can go to feel the spirit of our creator and be close to God. It is this continual search that keeps me fishing. Amergin, together with many other Irish poets throughout the centuries, brought the spirit behind the salmon into their poetry. To an Irishman, seeing a salmon in the line of a poem is almost as good as feeling one on the end of a fly-line. And so it is that the salmon tradition has been set forever into the Irish culture.

ABOVE: *Four Masters Bridge crosses over an excellent stretch of the Drowes River. The plaque and busts on the bridge, at Bundoran, commemorate four priests who wrote the first comprehensive history of Ireland. The Irish are famous for being excellent historians and, during the dark ages, St Patrick mobilized thousands of monks to keep Irish history and literature intact by recording all they knew, and storing it in their monasteries.*

THE IRELAND EXPERIENCE

In our travels throughout the world we did not stop in another place that was so thoroughly saturated in the fly-fishing tradition. In grocery stores, pharmacies, restaurants, and hotels we found a culture so totally dedicated to the sport that we felt no longer alone in being such fanatics.

In a restaurant, you would probably order salmon for dinner, and pay for it with bills that have poets on them, and coins that have fish. You can buy flies and tackle in just about any store you go to' and everyone is fly-fishing or dapping. This is an old form of fishing where fishermen use real mayflies as bait and let them sail from the end of a 25-foot long rod on very windy days. The fly just dances on the surface of the water, and can illicit some explosive strikes from aggressive fish.

After we got over the original culture shock that we felt having arrived direct from Bhutan, we were intoxicated by the tranquility and character of this ancient country. God never created a place that was more aptly suited to the pursuit of "gentlemanly" chalk-stream fishing.

The countryside embodies antiquity, beauty, and a seemingly timeless aura. Try to picture a rough landscape with large boulders and rocky, uneven hillsides; mountains and cliffs climb skyward right off the ocean, and castles sit atop any nearby knoll or precipice. Carpet the whole scene with a thick, luscious layer of deep green grass dotted with thousands of sheep and a few dozen lone herders with canes and sash chapeaux on their heads. This is Ireland.

Fishing amongst it all, you feel as though you have fallen into a time warp. The sheep graze about you, and very old milk trucks drive up and down the old roads. Birds of prey hunt rabbits from high above you, and you feel out of place with all your modern fishing equipment. Be ready to take a small step back and enjoy the timelessness of this beautiful land.

TACKLE AND GEAR

ROD AND REEL

Your selection of rods will depend mostly on what you will be fishing for. While we were in Ireland, we fished for salmon, sea trout, and brown trout. The brown trout we caught while fishing in large loughs. These lakes had tremendous mayfly hatches while we were there. Some of the mayflies were three or four inches long. The fishing was with 9-weight rods. We would blind cast around fallen structures

LEFT: *Doolough, another lough near Delphi Lodge, is best fished from these old rowboats. Many times the salmon follow predictable paths through these loughs, and being in a boat to get* *out to those paths is a tremendous advantage. Often, it can become tremendously windy, and these boats are built extremely heavy to remain stable and true in the elements.*

and trees in the water, and strip the flies home. We never did any mountain-stream trout fishing that would necessitate a light rod, but it does exist in Ireland. All our trout fishing was from boats in wide open lakes.

The salmon fishing can get very tiring, because you will cast a great deal before landing a fish. So it is helpful to have a good stiff rod that will allow you to make long roll casts, and simple one-movement overhead casts. I used my 9-weight here as well, and it was enough. Unlike their Scottish neighbors, the Irish do not seem to enjoy spey casting. We only saw one person doing it, and she was a visitor. However, spey casting here would be very effective, and easy on your arms. You will get longer casts and many more of them. I used my 15-foot 11-weight rod a lot of the time. It takes a long time to catch these salmon, and every cast has to count. So, open up the rod room, and pick a winner.

LINES AND LEADERS

For almost every fishing situation in Ireland, you will want a weight forward floating line on any of your single-handed rods. You will want to punch out a long cast, let it swing downstream, strip, and then cast again. Use all weight forward lines.

Most of the rivers we salmon fished in Ireland were very slow, so I always used a floating line. But, the water was unusually low, and it is good to have a sinking tip just in case your fly needs to get down in higher water. Also, for the trout fishing, a full sinking line may be a good idea. Depending on the temperatures in different parts of the lake, you may want to get your line down very deep to get at the fish. If you are going to use a spey casting rod, get a salmon taper line. In Ireland, it's a good idea to make this a floating line with a sink tip. That will help your fly to get just a little under the surface where the salmon are to be found.

THE FLY BOX

Just as in Scotland, there are hundreds of fly-patterns here, but they are all stimulators, as these fish are not interested in eating. In my opinion, a simple white or black fly will be sufficient.

In Ireland, we used mostly small treble hooks with the local pattern du jour tied to them. One fisherman claimed, "You have to use a dark pattern when salmon see it low against a shaded sun. A medium colored pattern is best when the sun is high or not shining, and a light or bright one with flash when the sun is behind the salmon."

This is all just theory, and more amusing than substantive, in my opinion. You have to use what gives you the best hunch. Some popular patterns are the Silver Doctor, the Bloody Butcher, the Rusty Rat, the Collie Dog, and the Undertaker. Any of these flies should work just fine. I caught two salmon with the Collie Dog.

"Yet, you can't mistake the sight of a salmon, any more than you can miss the sound of a secret."

ESSENTIAL KIT

The sun doesn't always shine here. That is a gross understatement. It is quite often very misty and rainy. You will be wise to bring good rain gear, and chest waders to protect you against the elements. Also, your hands can get quite cold and wet. If this bothers you, bring some good stripping gloves.

Aside from that, make sure you have a landing net when you go out. These are big fish with plenty of kick. A camera will help you prove your stories. And, an alarm clock will help you get up in the morning. It is usually very dark, and your hotel may not have an alarm clock.

BELOW: *The Ballynahinch River is a perfect situation for spey casting. In the deep, slow rivers of Ireland, it is often difficult to wade far from shore.*
In addition, there is quite often a lot of brush behind you. Spey casting is a perfect way to get your fly out to the fish.

PREVIOUS PAGE: *Ballynahinch River is an age-old salmon fishery. On this beat, an angler can chose from several casting piers that were probably built a hundred years ago or more. The rocks and the moss that line these Irish rivers are part of what give them their charm.*

OPPOSITE: *This rainbow trout, caught by a local angler, was lost and had got mixed up with the incoming salmon in the brackish salt water of the Drowes River estuary. Trout and salmon are both members of the same family of salmonoids, and some rainbow trout will even return to the ocean like a salmon. They would then be considered steelheads.*

Conservation groups can be contacted through:

*SOS c/o Graham Shaw
PO Box 69,
Galway, Ireland*

*FISSTA c/o Tommy Lawton
Rath-Healy
Fermoy Co. Cork
Ireland*

*TAFI c/o John O'Hare
21 Main Street
Kenmare
Co Kerry*

CONSERVATION WATCH

The following essay was composed by Peter Mantle, who is the head of Delphi Lodge, where we stayed. Throughout the whole of Ireland we did not come across anyone who talked more fondly about the world of salmon conservation. I noted at one point in my journal that Peter was the first person we met who was actually doing something about saving the salmon rather than complaining about it. He is a fine man and a superb conservationist.

"While Ireland can boast a vast network of lakes and rivers, many of them in pristine condition, the country is not without its problems when it comes to game fishing. Each of the three main species – the Atlantic salmon, the brown trout, and its ocean-running cousin, the sea trout – faces a significant threat.

In the case of salmon, there is still an extensive coastal netting industry, which intercepts up to 80 per cent of the returning summer salmon using monofilament drift nets. Happily, the earlier-running and larger spring salmon are now protected by a delayed start to the netting season. But the summer slaughter is massive and makes little economic sense.

The wild brown trout of Ireland's great lakes – Corrib, Mask, Conn, and many others – are still present in good numbers, but increasing levels of pollution from agricultural and industrial run-offs require urgent attention. There is no excuse in the modern era for slurry spillages, excess fertilization, and blanket afforestation around spawning streams.

But the biggest disaster in recent years has been the near extinction of the famous West Coast sea trout, once the most prolific of fish in the spectacular wilderness surroundings of Connemara, Kerry, and Donegal. The advent of intensive marine salmon farming in the mid-1980s brought with it an explosion in the population of a natural but nasty little parasite, the sea louse. These lice, billions of which are now present in most west coast estuaries, have infested the outgoing sea trout smolts each spring – with devastating mortality rates. Once-famous fisheries like Ballynahinch are now almost dead.

Irish anglers are up in arms about all three of these issues. A major campaign to force the Government to take action against the salmon farms is headed by a rainbow alliance of angling groups called Save Our Seatrout (SOS). The anti-driftnet campaign is being spearheaded by the Federation of Irish Salmon and Sea Trout Anglers (FISSTA), and the pollution problems are being tackled by the Trout Anglers Federation of Ireland (TAFI). All three organizations are up against tough opposition and badly need funds to support their lobbying."

JUST ONE OF THOSE DAYS
SCOTLAND

AT THE BERRIDALE RIVER, SCOTLAND

The forecast for the day should have read: hail and snow, intermixed with sunshine, gale-force winds, and the occasional passing hurricane. The morning woke me with sleet cracking against the window. The wind sounded like rushing water as it swirled through the town of Halkirk. I put on my clothes and stood by the window, contemplating. What a beautiful sight, I thought. The force and fury of just a minor storm. Coming from Atlanta, I have fond memories of dark skies and powerful storms. I watched the leaves whistling through the streets, and saw a cloud of spray lift from the top of the river.

Peering into a bend of water, I wondered just what the salmon must be thinking. It must be rather encapsulating, the wind and snow blocking out their view of the sky, leaving only a dimly lit passageway leading upstream into the darkness of creation.

LEFT: *Helmsdale River, Scotland.*

After a seemingly long breakfast, we got our gear together and drove up the river. We passed through gale force hailstorms, which would later give way to bright blue skies. It was difficult weather to fish in, but with the Atlantic salmon coming upstream, it would take more than the weather to stop me.

Casting conditions were oppressive. Even with the double-handed rods, the line would very often shoot forward and then stop dead in the air as if it had hit a wall – leaving you with only a bird's nest to show for your effort. Systematically untying each and every wind knot, rubbing together numb fingers, I stood alone, isolated beneath the vast and turbulent Highlands of northern Scotland.

Some non-fishermen would probably wonder what on earth we were doing there; what spirit of life could possibly keep a man standing before a river in such conditions? Just when you thought the sun might start warming you up, you find another snow storm being driven down upon you with 80-mph gusts. The weather here isn't always like this, but it was just one of those days.

One of those days, indeed, when the strength of your heart is brought to the limit. Sailing through the air on a thin and fragile line was a piece of myself going somewhere, with all my will power behind it. Sometimes, when it seems like everything is trying to stop you, you pass a point of no return. At this point your insides no longer question what you are doing; your constitution allows your muscles to relax and your mind to let go – dissolving itself into that vast universe of peace. Now is the time when your perceptions will make your memories. Letting not one blow pass you by, you stand forward and confidently offer the winds the chance to test you.

Throughout the world, this happens in small ways every day. It has happened in big ways from time to time throughout history, but the spirit behind both is the same – freedom and love. Gandhi was a fisherman, and although he lived his life in an entirely different context, he understood the emotions I feel on the river. In his *Talisman* he wrote, about one's actions toward one's fellow man, "Will it restore him to control over his own life and destiny? In other words, will it lead to self-rule… then you will find your thoughts and yourself melting away."

Here, between the banks of the river at my feet, flowed that spirit that allowed me to melt away for a moment. The wind became my voice howling over the river that runs right through me. The spirit of life and the freedom to live it were swirling around me from every direction. To know that feeling, with all of its strength and fury, gives me the peace of mind to understand how to love something.

I'm fortunate enough to say that I am in love. And despite the strength and fury of that feeling, despite all its complications, it is a calm body of water. It is a feeling that has peace at its core, and at its edges is this man, standing in the morning's snow storm, savoring the howling wind, and pushing forth into the

OPPOSITE: *The elements in Scotland can be quite harsh at times. Wind, snow, and rain can all whip up into some ugly concoctions. "A good Scotsman," as they say there, doesn't let it bother him. A good Scotsman doesn't need a lot to stay warm, and drinks whisky or sloe gin at lunch. This attitude comes from the strong constitution it takes to live north of the Highlands. Here, in Halkirk, we fished Loch Beg like good Scotsmen.*

'It was just one of those days when the

strength of your heart is brought to the limit.'

PREVIOUS PAGE: *A brief moment of sunshine reveals the true character of the Scottish scenery. Everything looks as though it's been there for centuries, and it has – the river, the buildings, the rocks, and the fields. Here, we fish the Thurso river for salmon resting above the rapids.*

world, knowing that nothing can make him give up and go home. God, if only I could love her more. If only there were guarantees that as surely as the river pushes forward, the spirit that keeps us fishing – that spirit that does not accept retirement – will flow on forever. Yep, it was just one of those days when you really understand what it means to be alive.

A BRIEF HISTORY

Trying to trace back the origins of Scottish fly-fishing is like trying to write a book on the history of humankind – they go all the way back to the beginning. Many of the literary references relating to angling in the very early days have only recently been rediscovered and analyzed. A scholar could spend years traveling to museums, libraries, and private collections throughout the European continent in an attempt to find the source of the original "fly-fishing-for-salmon fountain."

I have come across dozens of documents and pieces of literature, many of which contradict each other. But one fact remains – the roots of our modern day form of fly-fishing come from ancient Britain. Today, the further north you go in Britain, the greater the fishing culture.

To start at the beginning, fishing hooks have certainly been in existence for 30,000 years. Archeological digs in countries along the Pacific Rim and in the Middle East have proved that fishing goes back to the earliest days of mankind. The first reference I have found relating to artificial fly-fishing comes from Macedonia around 200 AD. Aelian, a Greek author, wrote of a speckled fish that would rise when he would "fasten red wool around a hook, and fix on to the wool two feathers that grow under a cock's wattles, and which in color are like wax."

Many of the first literary references to fishing came from Macedonia and the eastern Mediterranean. Cleopatra, who inherited the Egyptian throne in 51 BC, was actually Macedonian. She was immortalized in William Shakespeare's *Anthony and Cleopatra* for her trick of sending divers down under the boat of her lover to attach fish to his hooks on a slow day. Such women cannot be found these days! Around the time of Cleopatra and the Caesars, fishing became a pleasure of country living. Ancient pictures indicate people fishing leisurely along the banks. The ancient author Mariel wrote of "…the joy of feeling a fish struggling on the end of a vibrating line."

Over the centuries, the Roman Empire expanded throughout Europe, reaching as far north as Scotland. In 122 AD, the Emperor Hadrian built Hadrian's Wall along the northern border of England, in what is now Northumbria. This wall still stands, and is now the gateway to Scotland. With their love for idle fishing, the Roman nobility must have found the British countryside ideal for passing the time. In fact, Britain was so perfectly suited to gentlemanly country sports that the culture has never left the British Isles and these pursuits have become part of its national identity.

Still, in these ancient days, the British were a very superstitious nation. Many people were afraid of the dark waters and the mysteries they held. In fact, for almost a thousand years, from Roman times until the arrival of the Normans, there is hardly a single reference to any sports taking place upon a river or in the field. One of the earliest surviving written manuscripts in English was written around 720 AD. This epic poem, entitled *Beowulf*, reveals the attitude of these early pagans toward the water. Confronted by Unferth, son of Ecglaf, the hero Beowulf is forced to defend his reputation of bravery by recalling an instance in which he actually swam in the ocean for a competition! But rather than foolishly going in unarmed, "We had naked swords, strong in our hands…". He also wore chainmail to protect

BELOW: *There is a channel of deep water that cuts across Loch Beg like a lazy "S." We are fishing that channel from a boat, for better access to the fish. The hull of this boat is made of concrete to keep it from drifting in the howling winds. Loch Beg is considered one of the gold mines along the Thurso River.*

himself from monsters and "whale-sharks." Later in the poem, a deep blue lake is mentioned as home to the evil mother of the monster Grendel. As Beowulf traversed the lake, "many monsters attacked him in the water, many a sea beast tore at his mail-shirt with war tusks, strange creatures afflicted him."

However, around 1100 AD there was a perceptual shift in the human attitude toward the outdoors. People were no longer so afraid to seek pleasure in the natural world. The sport of fishing, which had previously been enjoyed by the Romans and Egyptians, began to flourish and take on an entirely British identity. In 995 AD, Aelfric, Archbishop of Canterbury, wrote *The Colloquy of Aelfric*, the oldest English fishing literature I have been able to find.

The Boke of St. Albans was published in 1496. This book contained the first major landmark in angling literature, *The Treatyse on Fysshynge with an Angle*. The authorship of this book is attributed to a shadowy female figure named Dame Juliana Berners. Little is known about her except that she was a sister in a local convent. This publication was the first to prove that a major fishing tradition was alive in the British kingdom. It also contains the first mention of catching Atlantic salmon with a fly:

"For by cause that the Samon is the moost stately fyssh that ony man maye angle to in fresshe water. Therefore I purpose to begynne at hym. The samon is a gentyll fish: but he is comborous for to take. For comynly he is best in depe places of greete ryvers: And for the more parte he holdyth the myddys of it: that a man maye not come at hyme. And he is in season from Marche unto Myghelmas (Michaelmas or Christmas). In wyche season ye shall angle to hym with thyse baytes whan ye maye gete theym. Fyrst with a redde worme in the begynnynge and endynge of the season. And also wyth a bobbe that bredyth on a water docke. And he bytith not at the grounde: but at ye flote. Also ye may take hym but it is seldom seen with a dubbe at suche tyme as whan he lepith in lyke fourme and manere as ye doo take a troughte or a graylynge. And thyse baytes ben well prouyd baytes for the samon."

What she calls a "dubbe," we know as a dry fly. Later in her book she describes twelve essential dry flies. She also goes into great detail about how to rig a rod and a line, how to tie a fly, and how to approach and catch all types of fish. She was not writing about some sort of experimental art here; she was describing a sport that had been continuously developed for many years. She also alludes to other works on the subject from previous centuries.

LEFT: *The houses and buildings in the country-side here are all strong stone structures that look as though they could withstand anything. Here, in Glenshee in the Grampian mountains, we see some of the world's most rugged and beautiful terrain. For centuries, this area was a battleground for Scottish clansmen fighting against each other, and against the English.*

ABOVE: *Taking a break along the Thurso River. The tackle used in Scotland is some of the best looking of all fishing tackle. The large arbor spey casting reels, thick 14-weight line, and a double-handed rod are all part of the experience.*

The *Treatyse* has since gone down in history as the founding document on the art of fly-fishing. Then, less than 200 years later, the most famous book on fly-fishing ever published came out, and it remains in print to this day. *The Compleat Angler*, by Izaak Walton describes the many aspects of fly angling in tremendous detail. Although he does not actually talk about taking salmon very much, his techniques of delivering the fly to the water are almost certainly those that were being used on the salmon rivers at the time.

With the publication of *The Compleat Angler* in 1653, the sport of fly-fishing took a permanent place at the table with all the great outdoor sports of the world. From this time onward, the Scottish and the English settled the furthest ends of the world, setting up some of the most prolific fisheries in the world as they did so.

For example, James Bruce, from Stirling in Scotland, was an explorer who set out in 1768 to discover the source of the Nile. Being a keen fisherman, he brought with him flies and long salmon rods. Wherever the Scottish and the English people went, they seemed to take their fishing gear with them. And not only the fishing gear — the fish, too. The world-class fisheries in Tasmania and Southern New Zealand are all descended from Scottish stocks in the River Wey and other spots.

The fly-fishing tradition in Scotland and England is one of the oldest in the world; and it is the root from which all modern fly-fishing began. Dame Juliana and Izaak Walton immortalized this tradition, and you can still feel that spirit every time you look down from a Highland mountainside or walk across one of their lush green fields. The echoes of a thousand years of fly-fishing resound.

From there, the tradition has blossomed throughout the world. The Americans have taken part of that tradition, developed it, and made it their own. One cannot talk about Atlantic salmon fishing without mentioning Lee Wulff, the godfather of North American salmon fishing. And in Scotland there have been too many legends to mention, some still living today. Alistair Gowans, with whom we fished for several days, is one of them. Hopefully, there will be many more.

THE SCOTTISH EXPERIENCE

No group of people on Earth are more animated, or opinionated, about fly-fishing than the Scots. Their methods and traditions make up what is possibly the oldest fly-fishing culture on Earth, and the regality of this claim gives the fishing here a certain loftiness. It certainly stands apart from all others.

Every time you go fishing here, you feel as though you are taking a small step back in time. There are great numbers of trout, but the real trophy is the Atlantic salmon (*Salmo salar*), and the name of the game is spey casting.

The days are filled with long, arching roll casts, using a double-handed rod to punch a sprinting loop over the water. Even the flies have an ancient feel to them. Although most people use more modern flies these days, every lodge and bedroom is adorned with the old Atlantic salmon flies that some of the more elderly anglers still use to great effect.

Do not be surprised if your ghillie shows up in a tweed coat with a flask of sloe gin or Scotch whisky in his creel. In fact, be surprised if he doesn't! Things here are very traditional, the fishing methods have been tried and tested for hundreds of years, and they are ingrained in a way of life and an attitude toward the sport. My father was born and raised in Scotland; so being half-Scottish, I was completely drawn in

BELOW: *The Atlantic salmon can be a tricky fish to land. A fresh one may have several strong runs in him. Sometimes, when you get one close to shore, just before you net him, he might thrash his head one last time and break your line or spit the hook. Usually, you can tell once you've hooked one whether it is a fresh fish from the ocean, or one that has been in the river from the previous year, a kelt.*

PREVIOUS PAGE: *The falls on the Forss River, near the Forss House Hotel. Jamie MacGregor, the proprietor of the hotel, explained how fish from each river have evolved differently depending on how the river their ancestors swam up is constructed. On the Forss River, natural selection weeds out the fish that are not well equipped to leap up these falls. As a result, a Forss River salmon may jump more than other salmon when hooked.*

by the aura of this magnificent country. In the mornings we would eat a hearty breakfast of black pudding and eggs before heading out to the misty rivers. The evenings were spent dining in the cosy pub at the Ulbster Arms Hotel learning about fine malt whisky and hearing the day's stories – all of them about salmon, of course - bouncing around the tables and the bar.

The days are filled with an incredible flood of fishing concentration. Unlike fishing for trout or bonefish, the Atlantic salmon hits you by surprise and doesn't give you a moment to recover. After countless casts, and hours spent staring into the darkest of the cold water, you begin to think that there is nothing left in these rivers. Then, without any notice, an enormous fish will leap right out of the water, breaking the silence of the day. Just seeing it happen gets your blood pumping. And when one hits, it is like an owl swooping out of the dark night. There is no warning, and it hits in a big way, tugging your attention right out of your head. It is an amazing experience to catch a Scottish salmon.

Some of the best fishermen in the world live in Scotland, spending their time catching the salmon and studying its life-cycle. Alistair Gowans from Pitlochry is widely revered as one of the very top fishermen and fly-tiers in all of Scotland. His 150-foot casts, and his knowledge of salmon behavior (much of which comes from his son, who has a Ph.D. in salmon behavior), are unrivaled. If you can book him as a guide, you will be in for a tremendous experience. He taught me to spey cast on the Scottish Normark rods that he designed. People say of him, "You'll never find a finer fly-fisherman anywhere in the world, and he's a streak of luck like you've never seen."

And all of this happens in a setting completely unique to the Highlands. Unlike England, this is very rugged terrain. Large boulders and very mountainous bedrock underlie a thick, luscious soil with green grass as far as the eye can see. Sheep and cattle herds dot the landscape, and it is almost impossible to fish here without seeing many of them in the course of a day. In the spring, the sheep give birth just as the spring runs are starting to come up the rivers in good numbers. Most die-hard salmon fishers in Scotland say, "A good Scotsman prefers springers to those old, summer fish; not a shilling's worth of meat in the body."

There is a lot of talk about being a good Scotsman. Usually, the harder something is to do, the better a Scotsman you are for doing it. This includes drinking some painful concoction with lunch on the river, not wearing enough warm clothes, and of course, catching the biggest fish of the day. And, if it's a kelt (a salmon still in the river from the year before, usually much smaller, and recognizable by its pink gills), it doesn't count! In fact, if you catch a kelt, do not tell anyone – you won't be a good Scotsman! I, of course, caught plenty of them and enjoyed every minute of it.

TACKLE AND GEAR

RODS AND REELS

The most unique thing about the fishing here is the traditional style. Almost all Scottish fishermen use long double-handed spey-casting rods. They use this style to throw consistently long casts with one sweeping movement at a time.

I used a 15-foot 10/11-weight rod. The longer you can cast with these rods, the better. If you can spey-cast a line around 100 foot every time, you will be doing pretty well. Just make sure you practice a lot before you come. Every cast here must be perfect. If you cast straight across the river, your fly will come zinging across too fast. You want to cast it at 35–40 degrees downstream and let it drift across slowly. The ultimate cast will leave a nice bright fly floating for a moment above the fish's nose. Long, downstream casts to the opposite bank will maximize this effect.

BELOW: *From a bridge over the River Ericht, I watch Alistair Gowans cast into some very tight spots. "Ally" Gowans is known as one of the finest spey casters in the British Isles. He could just as easily throw 150 feet of line across the roaring River Tummel as he could sneak a cast under some over hanging limbs 30 feet away (as he does here). Learning the art from him was a pleasure.*

BELOW: *Choosing a fly beside the Tummel River, near Pitlochry. Deciding on a salmon fly can be a tricky business. Some people say it doesn't make any difference which fly you use if you get it to go across the salmon's nose.*

Others say there is a science to it depending on the height and position of the sun. I had the most luck with a Collie Dog.

Simple flies seem to work. White and black are good basics, but others prefer flashier colors such as blue, silver, and orange.

These spey rods will also allow you to make very powerful overhead casts with no false casts. You can pick the line up, and throw a very long cast with one smooth motion. A single-handed rod will work, but if you can learn how to use these double-handed rods, it will make your life quite a bit easier.

LINES AND LEADERS

Atlantic salmon, contrary to most people's belief, do not sit on the bottom of deep pools very often. Even out at sea, the salmon tend to stay relatively near the surface. The most effective line you can use is a floating salmon-taper line with a 10-foot sink tip. This was the ideal set up for almost every river we fished, as most were not very deep, and not very fast.

However, when we fished the Tummel River with Alistair Gowans, we needed number 3 or 4 fast-sinking lines, because in places the force of the water was very strong and the level got extremely high. Without some significant weight, the tension on the line keeps the fly too near the surface when the fish might be deeper resting behind rocks.

As for your leader, just make sure it is strong enough. These fish are very powerful, and they are not leader-shy. They strike out of aggression, and they fight with the same ferocity. I used nine-foot leaders tapered down to 15 pounds, and I found that this was sufficient.

THE FLY BOX

There are heated debates in this part of the world about the advantages and disadvantages of different flies. There are some very popular fly patterns, but some locals will say even of these, "I wouldn't go near th' bloody thing."

The fish are not feeding as they would at sea. Once they enter the river, they have enormous fat reserves to provide energy, and sometimes they will not swallow any more food for over a year. What you are doing is taking advantage of their aggressive, predatory nature, and seducing them into hunting your fly.

The most popular flies that we came across were the Willie Gunn, the Fast Eddie (named for the keeper of the Thurso River in the far north of Scotland), the black and white Collie Dog, and the Ally's Shrimp (designed by Alistair Gowans). These are all tube flies, and they were all we used in Scotland.

ESSENTIAL KIT

Dress warmly. Remember that you are a long way north, and the weather can be very severe, especially in the early part of the spring, when blizzards are common. However, what you wear will depend to some extent on where you are in Scotland, so ask your hosts for advice.

Wellingtons are very useful boots to have in Scotland, allowing you to walk around in the mud safely and cleanly. Many of the rivers are small mountain streams that you won't need to wade. On one occasion I fished one in my kilt and boots. You could also bring hip waders. Not many locals wear chest waders, unless they are going to a deep river. Just find out which rivers you will be fishing, and ask what will be appropriate.

Landing nets for Atlantic salmon are very large. Do not bother bringing your trout net – the salmon will simply laugh at it. Bring a large landing net if you can fit it in your luggage; otherwise make sure that your guide has one. The springers will kick an awful lot. Have fun!

CONSERVATION WATCH

The following piece on salmon conservation in Scotland was written for this book by Alistair "Ally" Gowans. Ally is widely regarded as a legendary fly-fisherman in Scotland. He is a world-renowned fly tier, and recently won an award for "Fly of the Millennium" with his "Ally's Shrimp." He is a consultant for rod companies around the world, and can spey cast a fly line 150 feet. He was our guide on the Tummel River, and you couldn't meet a more pleasant man.

"Wild stocks of *Salmo salar* are diminishing at an alarming pace throughout their extensive North Atlantic range. Historically there were populations in every country from Spain northwards to beyond the Kola Peninsula in Russia, on the eastern side of the ocean. On the western side, they inhabited rivers at similar latitudes in Canada and the USA.

Sustainable commercial fisheries, harvesting thousands of tons of salmon, existed during the last century with little apparent damage to stocks. However, the numbers started to fall in the 1970s, a trend that is continuing today with little sign of respite. Very few legal commercial fisheries now operate in Scottish waters, but the runs of fish returning home show little or no sign of recovery. If I had to cite a single cause for this, the only word that comes to mind is "man." Man goes about his pursuit of pleasure with little conscience or thought for the future, and it is probable that his activities will yet destroy planet Earth.

In common with many other species, salmon survived well until humans started causing environmental damage on an enormous scale. Much of this damage was, and indeed is, due to ignorance as well as an attitude that favors short-term gain over long-term considerations.

Each river has its own particular set of circumstances and associated difficulties, and it is hard to know all the factors that contribute to its particular fish stock problems. However, it is especially saddening that man's insatiable greed usually prevents the appropriate remedial action being taken once a river's specific problems are known and understood.

If the salmon's demands for clean rivers are to be satisfied, we must appreciate that watercourses reflect the state of the land through which they flow. If we are good caretakers of the catchment, the rivers will remain healthy and bursting with life. If we abandon precaution in our haste for short-term gain, irreversible changes

"Ally Gowans — you'll never find a finer fly-fisherman anywhere in the world, and he's a streak of luck like you've never seen."

will occur, species will be lost, and the world will become a very much poorer place. Land and forest practices can have serious detrimental influences on watercourses. Drainage creates fast runoff from rain or snowmelt, with increased siltation and damage to the bed and structure of rivers during floods. During dry periods, greatly diminished flows result in the mean wetted area of the system being reduced and its productivity is seriously impaired. It is estimated that a quarter of a catchment's potential can easily be lost by this means alone. To exacerbate this problem, many of the chemicals used in farming, forestry, and other industrial and domestic activities cause pollution in different degrees, from total kill to varying levels of eutrophication. In some instances, the local ecosystem is forced to adapt, with the result that much of the indigenous flora and fauna is lost.

In the seas around the UK, and in the Atlantic Ocean, vast quantities of protein-rich fish are harvested, to an extent far beyond their natural replacement

BELOW: *Fishing the underwater channel in Loch Beg is a good bet in the quest for a salmon. It's also one of the most sought after beats on the Thurso River. As soon as the sun came out on our last day, our ghillie said we wouldn't catch any more salmon. The fish don't seem to like the sun, which might be why there are salmon in this part of the country! But a cool, overcast day with a good flow is a good recipe for salmon catching.*

PREVIOUS PAGE: *The estuary of the Naver River was a sight to behold as we drove west along the Scottish coastline. At low tide, the stream isn't much more than a shallow 30 feet wide. Then, at high tide it turns into a wide sea of water filled with salmon fighting their way into fresh water. Estuaries like this one are favorite ambushing spots for seals, who kill the salmon in large numbers for food.*

rate, to satisfy demands. This harvest is processed into fishmeal, oil for power stations, and food for cage-reared salmon and other aquaculture. It takes ten tons of food to make one ton of farmed salmon, and it takes three tons of wild fish to make one ton of fish food.

The impact of aquaculture does not stop there. Harmful poisons are used to alleviate the diseases and plagues of parasites that infest the farms. Fish are treated by literally pouring these substances into the sea cages. From here, they flow on the tides and continue to eliminate other species. Unfortunately, even these deadly potions do not reduce the harmful affect of aquaculture sufficiently to prevent wild fish being affected by its pests. Sea lice, a natural parasite of salmon and sea trout, exist in enormous densities around the salmon cages, infecting juvenile wild fish with an excessive parasitic burden, and often disease, as they head for the ocean. Many of the small fish perish as a result.

Salmon have adapted through thousands of years of evolution to suit the rivers in which they breed. Local groups of salmon are closely related, and they live in a specific part of a river system in order to make best use of it for breeding purposes. This is the key to their survival strategy, and it is dependent upon them retaining genetic integrity as intended by nature. Perhaps the most sinister consequence of aquaculture, or indeed artificial stocking with non-indigenous stock, is that these fish may interbreed with wild stock and destroy the traits essential for their life cycle success. Many of the Scotland's rivers that are relatively close to salmon farms are experiencing serious damage, if not extinction, of wild salmon stocks for this reason. The same thing is occurring on Canadian rivers.

RIGHT: *Salmon hatchlings developing at a spawning ground. A single salmon can produce thousands of offspring. However, less than 2 per cent of them will survive the trip to the ocean and back. The numbers of fish are dwindling every year due to commercial fishermen, growing seal colonies that eat the fish in hoards, and disease from salmon farms. Many once prolific rivers in the British Isles and Canada no longer have salmon.*

What of the future for wild Atlantic salmon? It is easy to become depressed by the multifarious problems that exist for the salmon, especially when these problems are merely a symptom of a more widespread malaise. However, *Salmo salar* is a great survivor, and if this magnificent fish is given a fair chance it will continue to grace our world for a long time to come. All that is required is for us to again make its environment suitable. It should not be forgotten that we share that environment. Just like the salmon, humans and most other species depend upon clean water and sustainable food sources for survival. If the salmon is at risk, sooner or later we, too, will become endangered. We must save the wild salmon in order to make the world a safe place for us.

Depressing as all this may sound, many Scottish rivers still have good runs of fish, particularly during the latter part of the season. The shortage of spring salmon is being addressed by voluntary catch and release that has been willingly adopted by some anglers and ignored by others. Incentives are being offered for the release of fish on some rivers to encourage the sportfishing ethos. Several conservation bodies are also fighting for our rivers, and there are signs that the reconstituted Scottish Parliament may be prepared to legislate to help save our rivers. It would be an enormous pity if the country that has contributed so much to salmon fly-fishing around the world should not do everything possible to retain its own salmon population. During the 19th century, apprentices indentured in the City of Perth were protected by contract to prevent their employers feeding them fresh Tay salmon more than twice a week, which graphically illustrates the one-time plenitude of salmon. If we all do our bit, we can save the salmon yet. But we don't have a minute to spare." – Alistair Gowans, Pitlochry.

To become involved, contact:

Scottish Anglers National Association
Caledonia House
South Gyle
Edinburgh EH12 9DQ
Scotland

The Salmon & Trout Association
Fishmonger's Hall
London Bridge
London EC4R 9EL

OCEAN JEWEL
THE BAHAMAS

KEY LARGO, FL, BAHAMAS.

The Bahamas was a new stop for us, and we had to start dancing to a new beat. Ever since we started our trip, we had been fishing river water; but getting onto the flats for bonefish was a whole different experience – mentally and physically. At the same time, I was returning to an environment that I feel at home in. I spend a lot of time with the sea, and I am very much at ease with a saltwater fly-rod. Furthermore, if I am not fishing, there is a good bet you will find me out sailing. I enjoy living with the tides.

Water and wind are my two favorite elements, because they make for good fishing, but most of all because they calm my mind and soul. The ocean is the home of these ancient partners, and their time spent together has been an incredible story of wonder, terror, love, and discovery. Everything you see around you originated in the ocean, and I believe it is to the ocean that we all belong.

LEFT: *Bonefishing from a skiff off Andros Island in the Bahamas.*

About 70 per cent of the Earth's surface is covered by water. For many of Earth's creatures it is a home; for others it is a means of transportation, to some it is a source of food. But to all who venture to contemplate her, she is a source of great wonder. Even the greatest achievements of human civilization are dwarfed to the point of triviality by the vastness and beauty of the oceans.

I have often wondered how we can sit on her shores watching the waves roll in, or soak in the moonlight gleaming off her surface, and never seem to get enough. No one can sit on a beach alone and actually want to leave it. The ocean has a hypnotic pull that seizes us with a grasp that is difficult to break. The ocean brings us closer to God.

Standing up to your ankles in saltwater is an incredible feeling. Waves roll by and flatten themselves into the sand. The water rushes past you, distancing you even more from the land behind. But each wave's escape is cut short, and it slides back around your feet and returns to whence it came. The pull of this return sneaks the sand out from under your feet, and each consecutive wave buries you more and more – bringing you closer to the sea.

Greek myths tell of sirens who would appear from the sea. These beautiful seductresses would stun their victims with their beauty and passion before luring them into the dark water, never to return. Whether it be the sirens, or our own search for the absolute, the pull of the ocean can be incredibly great.

Turning in the sand and facing the world behind you reveals so many things that you already know – your home, your life, the complexities and hopes that surround you. But returning to the sea, you find a world so awesome that the fear of losing yourself in it doesn't seem so bad. The horizon is so vast as to be almost infinite, and the water so deep and dark that it would appear to hold the answers to all things. Standing so close to a world this limitless is like standing on the threshold of existence, delicately skating along the boundary between creator and creation. What is out there?

We search for answers and solutions on the banks of this other world. Anything imaginable must be out there somewhere. Yet still, being unable to contemplate the idea of infinity, our minds look for connections between what we know and what we do not know. We search, we imagine, we dream.

If you could be a bird, what would you find if you set out to sea? Skimming across the tops of waves, miles and miles of water would pass below you, and you would catch glimpses of fish bubbling to the surface for sustenance

What would you find if you had the courage to fly on, further and further away from land. Would you discover a dot of land on which to rest your wings? Is there something different out there? Only dreamers would set off on such an adventure, dreaming as they went of a land that in itself would be a treasure.

Somewhere over the horizon, they would picture a place where islands emerge from the deep sea. Yellow and pink sands would surround these islands, and the water would be the color of blue sapphire. The temperature would be forever warm, and palm trees would fan the sea wind down upon you. Worries and fears would only be the subject of jokes from far away lands. Now, turn these dreamers into me and you, and add large schools of fish that are pound-for-pound the most powerful gamefish in the world. Put the fish in warm water and make them love a habitat that is shallow enough to walk around in all day. Welcome to the Bahamas.

When I looked out over the ocean's horizon as a kid and dreamed of far away beautiful islands and of setting sail to their shores, I was having a premonition of my trip to the Bahamas with Peter and Beverly, and now we are here. We had

BELOW: *Releasing a bonefish off Andros Island. Known as the "gray ghost," they are difficult to see in the water, and when walking across salt-water flats, it takes a keen eye and a good pair of polarized sunglasses to see one cruising. Their silvery bodies seem almost transparent, even in your hands. You could easily look right at one and not know it from a shadow on the sand or a ripple in the water.*

crossed the Gulf Stream from Key Largo and dropped anchor in the Bahamas for bonefish, and bonefish are what we found. This is a land that time, quite literally, forgot; a place of treasure and myths, with stories of Ernest Hemingway, Jimmy Buffet, Blackbeard, and ghosts that haunt some of the islands. What most people do here is bonefish, and that suited us just fine.

The bonefish is the most powerful fish for its size in the world. Yet, its most incredible strength lies in its ability to match its surroundings to perfection. In a body of water the color of fine gemstones, the bonefish swims like a rolling pearl over the shallow flats. The colors in which we found ourselves immersed could have come from the palette of Van Gogh himself.

All the while, as we prowl through the crystal clear waters with rod and reel, we are amazed by the powerful takes of these little silver fish. Fly-fishing itself needs no dreams, but if ever you could transport an angler from his stream and place him in an imaginary land of dreams and beauty, you would probably have him bonefishing at sunset in the Bahamas.

The sunsets in these islands are a little more extravagant than elsewhere, and as you look toward the horizon to where you once imagined far away lands, you realize that what you once sought is now all around you in shades of blue, yellow, and red. And when your reel starts to spin faster than ever before, or the clock above the bartender's head, back at the lodge, seems to beat just a few ticks too slow – just smile; changes in latitudes bring changes in attitudes, as an old Bahamian saying has it.

PREVIOUS PAGE: *When a bonefish gets this close to being landed it is not a good idea to pull too hard. Their large tails can propel them to 30 miles per hour in a split second. Bonefish usually have two strong runs in them, with a few smaller fights as they come in closer. After landing them, it is easiest to release the hook by turning the fish over on his back. They seem to be slightly tranquilized by this.*

OPPOSITE: *Peter's first bonefish, caught north of Norman's Cay in the Exuma Islands, was less happy to see him than he was to see it. A first time bonefisherman is always surprised at how powerful a small fish like this one can be. Within seconds of setting the hook, this fish can unload 75 yards of your line into the water.*

A BRIEF HISTORY

The *Albula vulpes*, or gray ghost, the magical bonefish that glides across thousands of the endless flats in the Bahamas, is a relatively new inductee into the exciting world of fly-fishing.

There is little doubt that as early as 1492 some of Columbus' crewmen caught a few bonefish as they dropped their line off the beaches of Guanahani, later known as San Salvador. In fact, so plentiful are these fish that they may well have been caught in many of the tropical oceans, such as the Samoan Sea in the southern Pacific or in the Indian Ocean near Mozambique, even earlier than history can record. Hawaiian scientists have identified their own species of Pacific bonefish, called the *Albula neoguinaica*.

No matter when or where this fish was first hooked, I'm sure the casual fisherman wading the shoreline or relaxing in a dugout got quite a wake-up call when the fish first hit. You won't often find a creature of this size that will fight as hard as the bonefish.

It is this incredible excitement that has lured thousands of saltwater enthusiasts to the Bahamas to catch this fish and its partners in the golden circle of the Grand Slam – the permit (*Trachinotus falcatus*), the tarpon (*Megalops atlanticus*), and of course the bonefish (*Albula vulpes*).

The history of catching these fish on the fly appears to go back farther than most modern fly-fishermen realize. The first writer I have come across who claims success was James Henshall. He described his fishing trip of 1878 in his *Camping and Cruising in Florida* (1884):

"…fishing with the artificial fly can be practised and enjoyed to the fullest extent, where fish are so abundant… For instance, I took crevalle of five pounds, sea trout of ten pounds, redfish of five pounds, blue fish of four pounds, "snooks" or sergeant fish of six pounds, bone or ladyfish of two pounds…"

A man named Maxie who wrote for *Forest and Stream* on April 8, 1896, also claimed to have caught bonefish. In his article he cited the correct scientific name of the fish. Furthermore, his description of the fight of the fish he caught matches that of the bonefish. He claimed that the "bonefish" mentioned by Henshall was only a "lady-fish." Maxie caught these fish with "a medium weight fly-rod with large gaudy salmon or bass flies."

From the following decades there have come several reports of men catching the bonefish on a fly. Holmes Allen was one such person, credited with a catch in 1924. Colonel L.S. Thompson also caught several at Long Cay in 1926. Saltwater fly-fishing soon became a recognized and important sport. In the late 1920s, a fishing club called the Bang Bang Club opened on Pot Cay in the North Bight of Andros. It was rumored to be owned by Al Capone, and it hosted several of the country's wealthiest families. The club operated for more than 30 years, and it was said to have the best bonefishing in the Bahamas. Joe Brooks, regarded by many as one of the finest fly-fisherman in the world for many years, first visited there in the early 1950s.

Shortly after the Bang Bang opened, several wealthy American families began arriving in the Bahamas on their beautiful wooden yachts. One of the most notable of these families was that of Henry Mellon. His family spent months every year sailing down the eastern coast of Andros. In the early 1940s, Mellon, together with his wife, Tiny, sailed his yacht into the Middle Bight of Andros. This trip was to be the first of many annual visits to the island. When the Mellon family arrived, they hired local guides from Moxey Town to take them bonefishing. From this time onwards, the Moxey family has had a tradition of producing superb fly-fishing guides. They have opened a lodge that is still operating today. On one of the walls of the Moxey's Guesthouse and Bonefishing Lodge, you will see a faded picture of one of the old Moxey guides. He is holding a bonefish head whose body

OPPOSITE: *Mangroves, which form complex mazes of underwater jungles, are quite beautiful, but can be quite dangerous to the angler. Once hooked, a bonefish may make his first run into a jungle of mangrove trees. This usually means the end of the fight, because unless the fish is pulled out exactly as he went in, the tippet will snap after tangling around enough underwater branches. However, because of the protection they offer, bonefish will often be found feeding along the edges of the mangrove, as here, off Andros Island.*

was eaten by a shark as they were fighting it in. If you look at the picture, you will see that the head itself must be nearly a foot long, and possibly weighing as much as three or four pounds. I can only imagine the size of the whole fish, but I can venture to say it would have been a world record.

Many of these bonefish were caught while fishing for other, much easier fish, such as tarpon or jack. In 1947, Joe Brooks claimed to be the first person to take a bonefish on a fly intentionally. To record the event he took the *Miami Herald* sporting editor, Allen Corson with him to Islamorada, Florida. Although people had been catching the bonefish for years, this formal "first" in saltwater fly-fishing started a culture that has only been improved upon and perfected by the likes of Dan Blanton, Lee Wulff, Billy Pate, Flip Pallot, and, of course, Lefty Kreh – probably the most proficient fly-fisherman in the world today.

Following Joe Brooks' catch, the Bahamian Government, proprietors of more than "70,000 square miles of fishing that is hotter than a Calypso singer going to town," saw the potential of sport fishing in the Bahamas, and they hired Don McCarthy as Public Relations Director for the fishing division of the Bahamas Development Board. McCarthy, who had first brought Joe Brooks to the Bahamas, then proceeded to lure many more American fishermen to this Caribbean paradise. These visitors discovered multitudes of fish, perhaps not as large as some in the Florida Keys, but in numbers that, in some places, will frighten you.

One time, I was fishing alone with my friend Dale Hughes on a small deserted island in the Exumas. We were camping on the beach, and it was a beautiful spring day. Light cumulus clouds drifting by on cool May breezes across miles of fishing flats. As I was walking across one of these flats, the sky started to darken over as a cloud drifted across the flat. I figured I would take a break and change my fly. As the cloud started to pass over me, the sand turned from tan to gray, but strangely my head and body were still in the sunlight. It took a moment for me to realize my mistake. I looked up at the sky and with the movement of my straw hat, almost an acre full of startled bonefish swirled the water all around me so suddenly I yelped and fell over backwards. I have caught a few of these fish, but these "gray ghosts" never cease to thrill me.

PREVIOUS PAGE: *Bonefish cruise these crystal clear flats for the abundance of small crabs and shrimp that live here, but also because relatively few predators can fit into the shallow waters. Nonetheless, they can still find themselves pursued by small sharks and barracuda.*

RIGHT: *As the tide rises in ankle-deep water, it is a good idea to keep an eye out near the deeper, darker channels from which the bonefish will move in. They usually appear from nowhere and require a quick cast before they pass. Peter, in the distance, gets down on one knee so as not to startle them. The fish can sometimes swim right up to you as they search the sand for food.*

THE BAHAMAS EXPERIENCE

This is one of the greatest of all fly-fishing sports. Fishing the flats for bonefish and permit, and the mangrove areas for tarpon, is an incredible joy. Few other angling experiences give the sportsman such an electrifying rush as saltwater fishing. It is not the mellow angling experience you might find from a trout river, but one that fills the body with adrenaline. Few places on Earth deliver as well as the Bahamas. As the legendary Joe Brooks said in the 1950s, "My main interest when I first went to the Bahamas was bonefish, and at the Bang Bang Club I found myself smack in the middle of some of the best bonefishing to be found anywhere."

There are two methods when fishing for bonefish. You either wade a flat or stand on the bow of a skiff with a guide poling you around the flat. Bonefish like

BELOW: *The Bahamas were once used as mid-way point for shipping drugs from South America to the United States. Some of the smuggling planes were so overloaded they never quite got airborne before hitting a tree and having to circle around for a crash landing on the flats. Here, at a secret spot in the Exumas, barracuda and sharks circle a downed DC-3, once owned by famed Colombian drug lord, Carlos Lehder.*

to escape the bigger predators of the deep water by coming up into very shallow water when the tide is rising. Sometimes, you will see these fish in less than a foot of water, and I have actually seen a few squirm over a small exposed sandbar to escape a predatory barracuda.

Once on these flats, they are open game to the angler, but they can still be very difficult to catch. You will only see them in two ways. You may see them cruising the flats searching for small shrimp or crabs. Or, you could see them feeding in a stationary position with their mouths down in the sand, and their tails sticking up – very often right out of the water. The "tailing bonefish" is a sight no angler will ever forget. When you see it, your heart will stop. The tail is usually much larger than you would expect and is very indiscreetly shaking back and forth as the head below searches for food. The tail shines and sparkles in the sun, and often you will see more than one at the same time.

In both situations, the food they will take is the same, but your strategy to get it to them is different. When they are cruising, you will want to get the fly way out in front of the fish. When the fish is about to swim over it, you must strip it as though the fly is trying to escape. If done properly, the fish will take very aggressively. In the second scenario, the tailing fish is not looking anywhere but down into the sand beneath him. Sometimes, you can almost hit them with the fly, and they still will not see it. What you must do here is cast your fly just to the side of the fish's head. Let it sink to the bottom, and then strip it away from him. If you are lucky, he will see it or sense it, and start coming after it. If he does, do not stop, just keep stripping it, and if he does not spook… Wham! He will take it and run unlike any other fish.

Of course, the bonefish are still around even when they are not on the flats, but they are usually only caught in deep water with spinning tackle. Sometimes, on a falling tide, bonefish will cruise the deep banks just off the sides of the flats and you may be able to catch them there. But usually, if they are not on the flats, and you cannot see them, you can only catch them with spinning tackle.

When the flats are dry, your best bet is to go back to the beach or sit under a palm tree and enjoy the piña coladas. The fly-fishing experience in the Bahamas is very laid back. Your surroundings make for an incredibly sensuous experience. All the colors around you are pastel blues, yellows, greens, and reds. The smell of wet tropical flowers drifts through the towns, and warm breezes keep you relaxed all day.

It is an absolutely thrilling experience, but just make sure that whoever you are going with knows what they are doing, because it is also a very technical sport. Seeing the fish can be very difficult. Furthermore, you will often be casting to moving targets from a moving boat – more often than not, in the wind. A good guide can make or break a day.

RIGHT: *Nurse sharks, like this one off Andros Island, will hunt the flats for bonefish as soon as it gets deep enough to keep their gills submerged. Often times they will appear completely oblivious to humans until they feel the gentle poke of a fly rod on their back. Nurse, lemon, and hammerhead sharks can be seen throughout the Bahamas. They are some of the most feared and efficient predators on Earth.*

TACKLE AND GEAR

ROD AND REEL

There is nothing more exciting than landing a big bonefish on a light rod. If you get good, calm weather and plenty of fish to cast to (the ideal conditions) it could be a lot of fun to bring a 6- or 7-weight rod. These are powerful, strong fish, and they can give a 6-weight something it has never seen before.

I certainly cannot talk about saltwater fishing without mentioning some bigger rods, however. Most of the time, there is a stiff wind blowing over the water. And, like most things, the best opportunities you get are the most difficult. You are sure to see a big bonefish cruising straight upwind of you. In order to get at it, you will need a powerful rod to punch through the wind. Do not go to the Bahamas without an 8- or 9-weight rod. Not only are they better for distance, but they will also help you to battle with the wind.

Also, remember that bonefish are only one of the "Big Three." Permit and tarpon are also very powerful fish. The tarpon in particular can grow to be the size of a full-grown man. If you fish for big tarpon, you will definitely need a heavy rod of 9-weight or above.

This is really the only chapter in the book where it is important to mention reels. A good quality reel is vital for this type of fishing. Fish on the flats, such as the bonefish, absolutely explode when they take a fly. You may see a rush of water, and before you know it, the fish will have run as far as 200 yards or even more. This kind of stress demands a reel with a good drag system that will prevent it from overshooting and tangling up the line. Manufacturers such as Abel and Tibor make excellent salt-water reels. When one of my best friends first caught a bonefish, his reel unwound so fast that the line got stuck, and the whole reel exploded. He still has a picture with his mangled reel and a ball of fly line. Be sure to get the right equipment when you go, and be ready to manage your drag system when the fish takes.

LINES AND LEADERS

Bonefish are not particularly wary of seeing the leader the way trout are. What is important is using a leader that is strong enough for a tough fight, and thick enough to turn over flies that can sometimes be very big.

Bonefish will take your fly and run, often for well over a hundred yards. While out there, they may swim into the mangroves or knock the line on some rocks or coral to get away. A light line will snap early. A more significant line will give you a better chance of pulling the fish back to you.

BELOW: *A small crab clings to a submerged mangrove branch. You'll never see a crab's back toward you. They always advance and retreat with their claws between you and them. Although this one would be slightly too large for most bonefish, they are in danger from other predators, such as gulls, who carry them high into the air and drop them on rocks and coral to crack them open. They are a delicious meat, and if caught properly from behind can make a tasty dinner.*

I would say a 10-pound leader is the minimum you should use. I actually prefer 15-pound material, because I have lost a lot of fish that have run off the flats and rubbed my line against a coral head.

Another important point is that when you are wading or poling the flats, you are certain to see several sharks and barracudas. These fish can also make for an amazing fight. The barracuda, especially, can become quite acrobatic in the deep water. I once saw a big one jump straight over a boat at the Moxey Lodge. Be sure to bring a spool of steel tippet material. Both of these fish have very big, sharp teeth. If you see one and want to try and catch it, it is important to first tie a six-inch piece of steel onto your leader

THE FLY BOX

Bonefish and permit like to eat shrimp and crabs. There are hundreds of variations of these crustaceans, but a simple selection of a few crustacean patterns will be

BELOW: *John Wayne, one of the top guides in Moxey Town, displays his handiwork with this nice barracuda. These fish can put up enormous fights, and leap in perfect arches 5-6 feet out of the water. Their jagged teeth necessitate wire leaders, and delicacy when removing the hook from their mouth. This one was going to be eaten by the locals, but it is not a good idea to eat barracuda, as their meat can contain dangerous bacteria called Ciguatera.*

sufficient. Colors can be important. I think simple, subdued colors are the best. Light yellows, pinks, browns, and oranges work best. A Crazy Charlie with a light brown body and some tan feelers is sure to work.

The Anderson's McCrab is one of the most productive crab patterns I have used. Bonefish, if they take it, will do so very aggressively. A couple more for your fly box are the Bonefish Special and the Snapping Shrimp – both very good shrimp patterns for shallow, grass flats.

It is important to bring flies of various sizes and weight. In very shallow water, you will want a light fly that won't drag through the sand or get caught in any sea grass. However, a deep flat will necessitate some flies with heavy steel eyes that can get down to the fish in a hurry.

No one pattern will work well all the time. Sometimes these fish will respond better to big flies and sometimes to small ones. Sometimes, they like crabs, and sometimes they like shrimp. It is important to experiment, and follow the advice of your guides.

Do remember to bring some big Deceiver-type flies with some flash in them for the purpose of attracting barracuda, sharks, and maybe some reef fish that interest you. Barracuda will attack a 20-pound fish, so there is no fly too large. Just make sure you can throw it.

ESSENTIAL KIT

Polarized sunglasses are probably the most effective tool you can have when fishing the flats. They reduce the glare on the surface of the water so you can see the fish below. Without them, you will be blind casting. Your guide can always act as your eyes, but you must be able to see for yourself.

The Bahamas are in the tropics and the sun is extremely strong. You are going to be out on the water all day long, which magnifies the strength of the ultra-violet rays, so bring strong sun block and a hat to protect your ears, neck, and face.

You will also note that most of the local guides choose to wear long shirts and pants. This is smart. If you get some very light, white pants, and a thin shirt, you will be able to cover your body. If you wear light colors such as white, you will not get hot. This may seem to take the fun out of being in the sun, but you will not regret it when you see the sunburn some people get.

Several manufacturers make ankle-high wading shoes. These are to protect you from stepping on sea urchins and stingrays – both of which can give you very painful damage. One spike from a sea urchin may immobilize you for the whole trip. Stingrays, sea urchins, and shells are all over salt-water flats, so it is best to be safe rather than get a nasty injury.

CONSERVATION WATCH

The Bahamas is not a highly industrialized nation. It is a quiet collection of hundreds of islands, which rest peacefully in the ocean. I would not cite it as one of the most ecologically troubled destinations we visited. The air, water, and land throughout most of the country is absolutely pristine.

However, despite their good luck, they do have some important ecological and environmental concerns. Motorboats can produce significant pollution problems if not maintained properly, and inconsiderate tourists still leave trash strewn across the beaches and empty toxic wastes into the water.

There are about a dozen national parks throughout the Bahamas, and their preservation is one of the most important concerns for the country. No fishing of any kind is allowed in these areas, and nothing can be taken from the reefs or sea bottoms. The area is totally protected and left to be seen by the rest of us as an example of an unspoiled tropical ecosystem.

In the Pelican Cay Land and Sea Park in the Exuma Island chain, there are tremendous undersea caves, and abundant coral reefs with hundreds of species of fish. The Abaco islands have a National Parrot Preserve where wild parrots still fly through the trees. There are also still herds of wild horses living in these islands, which need protection.

You will never cease to be amazed at what the Bahamas has to offer. Protecting this habitat – something we have failed to do in so many other places – should be a priority, so that our children and grandchildren will one day be able to visit these destinations.

To get involved and work towards protecting this magical land and sea, contact:
The Bahamas National Trust
PO Box N-4105
Nassau
The Bahamas
242-393-1317 Tel
242-393-4978 Fax

LEFT: *Once the sun goes down in the Bahamas, the bonefishing is over. However, anchored here at Gun Cay on our trip from Florida to Andros, I caught a 30-pound horse-eyed jack in the darkness. He swam in large circles around the boat for 20 minutes before coming in. There are seemingly endless numbers of beautiful fish in these waters, most of which will take a fly.*

THE LAND OF THE
MIDNIGHT SUN
ALASKA

BESIDE THE COPPER RIVER, ALASKA

Alaska stands apart from all the others. Like love, beauty comes in many colors. There are so many different forms and shades of love and beauty, and in Alaska, they shine bright. I remember one particular day when we came in from an aerial photographic shoot and were all almost physically stunned by the extremity of what we had just seen. It was more than just beautiful, or "really incredible." It pushed those things past the point where they can be so easily summed up. Its impact on us was so ferocious as to be almost peaceful. We had seen a place so awe-inspiring that I felt we had been touched by something that had never reached us before, something so peaceful and intensely real. Beverly told me that she "felt quite close to God up there." It was true, and it changed us all.

LEFT: *Fly fishing the Copper River, Iliamna, Alaska.*

I am a deeply religious person in my own heart, but I am not the kind of man who can be told what to believe. I shy away from people who try to frighten or trap me into sharing their beliefs. Mentally, I am a voyager, always in search of places that I love and can believe in. I have to discover for myself what brings meaning to my life. In Alaska, I found a great deal of that meaning, and I sailed home to a place that I love very deeply.

I have always been amused by the intricacies of my own mind. I grew up without a father, and that has had a tremendous impact on me. I spent a great deal of my young life learning how to be a man, without any male role models nearby from whom I could learn anything very productive. So I watched and observed people in the world, and I learned for myself who I wanted to be. I spent my childhood reading, making my own rules, rebeling, and, like most kids, adding what I could to the cause of raising hell. I scared and distanced myself from those that I love and who love me. I even frightened myself on a couple of occasions. But I discovered my limits and I learned about true friends; I found out what makes me happy, and I got my feet on the ground. And when I say that, at times, my own mind amuses me, I mean that the feelings that I have developed can sometimes me hit harder than I expect. It is as though different sides of my personality create opposing poles in my mind.

I have found that I feel most at home in the outdoors. I feel most alive when I can escape into nature. I am a fisherman, a hunter, and a sailor. I love casting into a river and searching for the pictures I paint in my dreams. I love stalking an animal for dinner, overcoming what I lack in speed and claws by using my mind and my bow and arrow. Even though I kill, I have the greatest respect and love for the animals of this world. Finally, I love handling the lines and ropes on a sailboat. I love to do these things, and I love them because I am constantly learning and developing in my own particular way. I push my barriers to the limit, and I try to be strong. What amuses me is the fact that in my life, as I try to be the man my father would be proud of, I can be knocked right off my guard by certain things that I find beautiful. When I feel close to things in life that are so near to my idea of God and Heaven, a tear can be brought to my eyes like a wind stirring a tree. I found that in Alaska.

To witness the Alaskan backcountry is, to me, to see a part of heaven brought to the Earth. In the mountains and valleys of Alaska, life, perfection, and purity are brought together in a way that is rarely found. For example, we flew to a lake in a crater that was created when a volcano exploded over a century ago. Cradled in the placid blue water in this little spot on Earth was a scene so ethereal as to be found in God's own den. Reflections of the rugged mountains and snow-capped peaks were shining perfectly around the cavernous icebergs floating in the water.

OPPOSITE: *The Venturi River snakes through some of the most beautiful country in the Aleutian Range. The rivers in Alaska are arguably the best in the world. They contain large trout, char, grayling, and all five species of Atlantic salmon. This rugged terrain, with glaciers, bears, mountains, and rivers is truly the last American frontier.*

As it passed beneath our wing, we were taken to a point beyond that of being amazed – to a sort of peace that they say comes before death. And just as I was realizing how blessed I was to be alive to witness something so perfect, our plane roared over the mountain and came down into a place where mother nature had really let her hair down.

As we flew along, the valleys were green, and wandering across them were the grizzly bears. The bears had not moved inland yet; they were all wandering the coastlines, waiting for the salmon to arrive. And, in this nature's morning, we saw real feeling alive in the wild. Some of the bears would stand, boldly opposing our loud intrusion. Some would run, or square off to the plane with their newborn cubs at their heels. One bear was absolutely immovable. He lay across the carcass of a beached whale that fortune had brought to his doorstep. No matter how many passes we made in the plane, he just placed his paws on top of his treasure, and stood firm as if to say, "I've found all that a bear could ever want, and I'll be damned if I'm going to move for you."

There were no hotels out there, no electricity, and no roads. There was only the bear, the bald eagle, the ocean, the mountains, and us – and, of course, the salmon. It was purity at its purest, and the world doesn't get much better than that. The wind in the tree that I spoke of was really beginning to blow.

Our flight that morning took us to Kodiak Island, in search of the Chinook salmon – the largest of all the salmonoids. It is probably one of fly-fishing's greatest accomplishments to land a "king" on a fly. If the weight of the fish – which may push 60 to 70 pounds – doesn't snap your line, his violent thrashing through the air may very well send your fly sailing back to the shore in failure. On top of this, the kings were just in from the ocean and still full of the strength and energy that they needed for the long trip upstream.

Joining us for the trip was a father with his young son. And during the course of the day, I ended up seeing something so touching that I will never forget it. No kings had been landed on a fly so far that year by anyone from the lodge. So, there was still a great deal of uncertainty about the success of the day to come. Yet, before the first 20 minutes were up, the young boy's father was hooked into a fish that woke us all up as the the father went running full-steam down the river with 30 pounds of muscle pulling him along in a swift current.

The young boy dropped his rod and darted like a shot after his father with the excitement and expectations only a boy that age can show. A good half-hour passed

LEFT: *A large grizzly bear protects his catch of the season, a whale that accidentally beached itself in Katmai National Park. The tides in Alaska rise and fall up to 30 feet in six hours, and a stray whale can easily find itself out of water in no time. Many bears will choose to live in the grass beside the high water mark. At low tide, they will go and scout the shallows for beached sea life.*

before they came back into sight over the hill; only they returned with a king in the father's hands, and the young boy by his side proudly accompanying his father, whom he admired so much. If I hadn't caught a fish for the rest of the day, just that sight would have made me happy, but there was even more to come.

A half-hour later, the boy finally finished touching and inspecting his father's salmon, and then he moved just downstream of his father and gave it a try with his own rod. On what must have been just his fourth or fifth cast, fate struck twelve, and with a large splash, the boy yelled to the world, "I've got a fish!"

This time, it was his turn in the sun. The fish he had on must have weighed half as much as he did. He fought that fish to the point of tears, and I honestly did not know what was going to happen. Thirty-five minutes passed, and the boy's

BELOW: *This man proudly shows off his beaming son's salmon in the Karluk River on Kodiak Island. A father and son fishing together is a terrific bonding experience. One can tell this nice Chinook salmon – also called a king salmon – is fresh in from the ocean because it has yet to turn red as they do before spawning after spending several weeks in fresh water. Fresh from the ocean, a Chinook will put up one of the fiercest fights in the world of fly-fishing.*

arms were so worn out. He was young, and in the midst of catching his fair share. Losing this fish would break him, but pushing on and trying to land it might break him too. This point might turn out to be one of his life's greatest memories and, no matter what was going to happen, the boy was not giving in. His father had put down his rod and gone to stand beside his son, his hand resting on the boy's strained back. Together they looked down the boy's tight line in anticipation, and for just a moment, time froze all around them. I blinked my eyes, and the image of father and son was imprinted on my mind forever.

The boy was fighting with everything he had inside of him, and his father stood proudly by his side. I do not think the father was thinking much of anything. He just had a warm and contented smile on his face. His young child was experiencing joy, and fighting one of fishing's greatest fights. The boy ended up asking for help, but the man knelt by his side, and told him that he could do it. He let him become a man on his own. If time had ended at that very moment, it would have ended in perfection.

I stood downstream of them and looked up. I smiled, as almost anyone would have done at a sight so perfect. I had been where the boy was at that moment, but I had been there alone. I smiled, not at memories of what I was watching, but at expectations of an amazing future, of bringing joy to the life of a child, my child. It was one of those times I laughed at myself. It was a touching moment, and the feeling shot right to my heart.

Like I said, it did not really matter what happened, but just to paint the moment perfect, the tired boy landed his fish and passed out on the shore for the rest of the day. I saw a day that boy would never forget. It was magic, and it could only have happened on a river.

Now, as we fly home from Alaska, our journey is ended. The longest cast has been made, and we bring back with us memories of some of the prettiest places on this Earth. Immediately behind us, Alaska stands like a great monument to it all. The bears still live in the coastal fields, and I know one still sits proudly over the whale he found on the beach. And there is a river bank on Kodiak Island that will forever contain the dim echoes of two people who landed a king salmon together. There is no doubt that a fisherman can find God in the river, but the feeling will stun him in Alaska. I think God felt like a bear, the day he created the land of the Midnight Sun.

"Fish," he said softly, aloud, "I will stay with you until I am dead." **ERNEST HEMINGWAY**, *the old man and the sea*

A BRIEF HISTORY

Before the Pacific salmon were ever fished, and long before pictures and scientists were around to record their behavior, the salmon were people that had previously lived on the Earth. Before they died, these people would go to the rivers and be transformed into salmon. Through this miracle, they could fulfill the magic of life's cyclical nature by coming back year after year into the rivers to provide food for their children and descendants.

Stories of creation, such as this one from the Makah Native American tribe of the Pacific Northwest, have been passed down the generations through oral traditions for thousands of years. In the same way that the Anglo-European culture expects the world to accept its version of creation, I think the world should accept the history of the Pacific Rim as it has been recorded by the people who have lived there. Since the beginning of mankind's presence in Russia and Alaska – a presence that recent archeological digs in far eastern Siberia suggest may be one of the oldest on Earth – the salmon and their seasonal migrations have been a source of magic, mystery, and a way of life.

To this day, many Native American tribes along the coast in Alaska and British Columbia take part in elaborate celebrations and festivals to honor the return of the first salmon of the year back into the rivers.

Elizabeth Woody, a well-known writer and artist from the Pacific Northwest, believes that the legend of the Anga Clan is another valuable piece of oral history:

"A very long time ago, one of the first members of this clan was a woman whose parents were taken from her in a tragedy. She was very lonely and used to wander down by the river in search of answers. One day, when the river was very high after a storm, she looked into the waves and saw a giant fish – first its tail, and then its head. As she watched the beautiful fish, it began to swim closer and closer to the shore.

"When the fish swam up to the rocks, it leaped out of the water, and began to roll up the hill to the woman's feet. 'This must be the master of the river,' she thought. As the fish approached, he said, 'Cook me quickly, eat me, and go to sleep.' Too frightened to run, the girl quickly followed the orders.

"After she had cooked the fish in a large pot and eaten it to the end, she fell fast asleep. Later that night, she woke up in the dark. She thought she was dreaming, and only the fire from the stove provided any light to the dim room. When she glanced around the room, peering into the night, she saw in one corner a giant salmon standing before her! The salmon came to her bed and transformed into a handsome, young man.

"She took him into her bed, and they lay as man and wife. They were happy together, and she gave birth to three sons. This made her happy, but as the children grew they longed for the company of others. So the family moved up the river to be nearer other people. The children developed strong friendships with others, and grew into three very handsome young men. 'So you see,' the woman told the others, 'our clan descends from the salmon.'"

While it may seem incredible to outsiders, these are the stories told and believed by many native people of the Pacific Rim. Just as we believe in our God and his miraculous deeds, they believe that the salmon is an expression of the gods. It is a fish whose meaning and power is greater than the limits of science will allow. To these people, the history of the salmon has been one of respect and celebration. It is a fish whose life has been the embodiment of nature and creation.

This history, however, has been forced to undergo some changes. The white pioneers and frontiersman did not see the salmon in the same light as the Native Americans who lived on the Pacific Ocean. The first settlers brought their knowledge of fly-fishing west with them, but were frustrated by the behavior of the fish. One western correspondent writing in July, 1852 under the byline of "Chinook" wrote the following passage in *The Spirit of the Times* magazine:

BELOW: *A nice Alaskan rainbow fights a lucky fly-fisherman in a crystal-clear, freestone river. The rainbows here get so large because, in addition to their regular diet, they feed off the millions of salmon eggs falling from the female salmon, and as the salmon die after they spawn, their meat fills the river with protein and fat for the other fish. Some experts believe that the strain of rainbow trout in Lake Illiamna produces the largest rainbows in the world. They act like steelhead, as they spend most of the year in the lake and then follow the salmon up into the rivers to feed and to spawn.*

"After reaching fresh water, the salmon of the Columbia [River] no longer feeds, as is the case with the European salmon, and no persuasion will ever persuade it to rise to a fly, a circumstance perhaps we are indebted to the peaceful settlement of the boundary question; for it is said that the officers of the British Man-of-War *Modeste*, which was sent at about that time to look around, became highly disgusted, and that Capt. Gordon wrote home to Lord Aberdeen that the d----d country wasn't worth having, for the salmon would not bite." However, the settlers soon discovered how to catch the salmon on flies.

One of the first things these tough, entrepreneurially-minded people noticed was the sheer abundance of salmon. Indeed, it was very difficult to miss. When explorers Meriwether Lewis and William Clark first arrived on the Columbia River in 1805, Clark remarked: "The multitude of fish is almost inconceivable. The water is so clear that they can readily be seen at a depth of 115–120 feet. But at this season they float in such quantities down the stream the Indians have only to collect, split, and dry them on the scaffolds."

By the end of the 1800s, these new, white Americans saw the potential profit of packing this easy multitude of salmon in cans and selling it to the settlers. The first of these canneries was built by Puget Sound in 1877. Salmon became so popular a commodity that the Native American's rights to the rivers banks were reduced to being no more than a nuisance. Although The Treaty of Neah Bay (1885) gave the Native Americans the right to fish "at all usual and accustomed places," by the end of the century, these laws were being ignored by the cannery owners, who chased the Native Americans from the riverbanks with guns.

After one such event, in 1897, the people of the Lummi tribe brought a suit against the canneries in the case of US vs Alaska Packers Association. Despite the rights granted to the tribes in The Treaty of Neah Bay, the courts awarded victory to the canneries, citing the importance of the salmon industry to America. Later that year, the Washington legislature revoked all Native American rights to fishing in Puget Sound, and all saltwater fishing within three miles of the mouths of all its tributaries. The beginning of the end had finally arrived.

Soon, salmon canneries were popping up all over the Pacific coast. Salmon was a popular commodity, and Americans were eating it with increasing frequency. During World War I, the industry boomed, as the American GIs were fed on huge quantities of canned salmon. When these men returned home with a taste for the fish, it became part of the American diet, drastically reducing the salmon runs on rivers from California to Alaska. The native tribes could see their livelihoods disappearing, and attempted to stop the frenzy, but the Great Depression and World War II raised the demand for canned salmon to new heights. In 1945, over 100 million fish were taken from Alaskan waters. Finally, in 1953, as people came to

their senses and realized what was happening to the ecosystem, the President of the United States declared the fishing communities of Southern Alaska a disaster area. With statehood in 1959, the Alaskan people finally began to gain some control over the situation. Certain methods of fishing, including the use of huge fish traps, were outlawed, and slowly the runs improved.

Today, the Department of Fish and Game in Alaska practices in-season management. This means that the Department can shut down certain rivers and fisheries at an hour's notice if a problem with the runs becomes apparent. Luckily, many of the dams that have been proposed in order to generate hydroelectricity from Alaska's powerful rivers have never come to fruition, although such dams have been built on the mighty Columbia River in Washington State, where the situation has already caused the extinction of several runs of salmon, and is endangering several more.

ABOVE: *Below a swift rapid in Amanda Creek on Kodiak Island, sockeye salmon would rest in great numbers in this dark, deep pool. It is a great place to drift a fly across their nose, where they will strike at it out of habit or annoyance.*

Once they have entered fresh water, a Pacific salmon will never eat again. But the fat they have stored up gives them enough energy for this fisherman.

For more than 50 years now, adventurous fly-fishermen have been going to Alaska to witness the magical spectacle of the salmon runs. Although the runs appear to be so plentiful that many people kill everything they catch, I like seeing the lone fly-fisherman who thinks that no one is watching, but still takes great pleasure in releasing a caught fish to swim for a few more days. Alone we stand watching the salmon disappear up the mountain; what a world in which we live.

BELOW: *The Kijik River is one of the best rivers in Alaska for grayling. So few fishermen have seen them, they will sometimes swim into the eddy behind your legs to rest. Here, I get my last cast of the day.*

THE ALASKA EXPERIENCE

There is probably no place on Earth where a fly-fisherman's dreams can be so fully realized as in Alaska. You are likely to catch more beautiful fish here than anywhere else I have been. We were in Alaska in June, and caught three species of salmon,

four species of trout, grayling, Arctic char, and pike. It is absolutely mind-blowing. Grayling and Arctic char are not as common these days as in the past. They are a real treasure, and yet we caught dozens of each of them – so healthy and beautiful. You really do feel closer to God up here. The air and water are so clear you feel high just being amongst it.

The details of the fly fishing here are the same as anywhere else. You will be wading cold rivers and streams, and fishing strategically for your target. You will have a box of flies, a strong leader, and a good rod. The real difference is in the big picture – and it is a very big picture. Alaska is real rugged terrain. The mountains here are enormous, with thousands of miles of crystal clear rivers just streaming down the sides. There is an abundance of fish and aquatic insects in these rivers that is hard to equal almost anywhere else. It is absolutely pristine.

In addition to the world-class trout fishing, people come to Alaska in search of the Pacific salmon. Five of the seven species are to be found in North America: the largest of these is the Chinook or king salmon (*Oncorhynchus tshawytscha*), which weighs an average of 24 pounds and can weigh up to 50 pounds; the others are the chum (*Oncorhynchus keta*), weighing in at an average of 12 pounds, the sockeye (*Oncorhynchus nerka*), the coho (*Oncorhynchus kisutch*), and the pink or "humpy" salmon (*Oncorhynchus gorbuscha*), so called because of the sharp hump it gets along its back when spawning.

These fish are born in fresh water gravel beds, and swim to the ocean when they are only a couple of inches long. When they return, one to five years' later, they are fully-grown. They will only spawn once, and they die soon after, having laid and fertilized their eggs. Their bodies slowly fall apart and become a vital food source for insects, fish, and other forms of aquatic wildlife.

One of the fish that eats the shedding pieces of the dying salmon is the rainbow trout (*Oncorhynchus mykiss*). In a great number of the Alaskan lakes and rivers, these fish follow the spawning salmon, eating their flesh and eggs once they have spawned. As a result of this rich diet, the trout here can reach enormous sizes. The average fish we caught was over three pounds, and the rainbows can be quite acrobatic opponents.

The salmon come up the rivers as voracious silver fish ready to leap the most powerful rapids and give birth to a new generation of fish. As they come out of the ocean and push their way up streams and into lakes during the summer and fall, they undergo a fantastic transformation. Their skin turns a deep red, the color of a rose. They become increasingly stoic and determined, and will never eat again. Their insides are so full of hormones and eggs, that their throats will not even allow food to pass. They can only be tempted to take a fly as an act of aggression if it passes too close to their face.

Meanwhile, during all this excitement, you will be surrounded by one of the most diverse collections of wildlife anywhere in the world. Just as the salmon begin to make their runs in the spring, the grizzly bears start to come out of hibernation to greet them in the fresh water. You will often come across grizzly bears fishing, or watching you fish, all along the banks of the rivers.

Bears love everything about salmon. Some of them catch the fish with their claws; some of them catch the fish with their mouths; some even hold their breath and disappear under the water to eat them like sharks. I have even heard stories about bears watching anglers from the woods, and when the fisherman hooks into a fish, the bear will come storming out to eat either the fish or the angler if he doesn't drop his rod. Using the line, the bears will pull the fish into the bank. Even more amazing than this, I once saw a grizzly bear catch a whale! While we were flying to Kodiak Island one day, there was a great commotion on the beach below us. Circling back, we found a group of grizzlies dining on a beached narwhal. It made for an amazing picture, not to mention food for thought about life and death in Alaska, and the irregularities in the world of Nature.

BELOW: *Arctic grayling have largely disappeared from most of their historic habitats around the world, such as Britain and parts of the continental United States. But looking at this grayling in the Kijik River in Alaska you would never know it. They are so abundant that in many situations you can sight fish and choose the ones you like the best.*

On other days, we relaxed on smaller streams in the mountains, spot fishing grayling or casting dry flies to Arctic char. Not a day goes by in Alaska when you don't thank Mother Nature for everything you have been given. Be ready for the experience of a lifetime.

TACKLE AND GEAR

ROD AND REEL

This is the place to open up the closet and bring out all of your favorite gear. You will need a full range of everything from rods to reels to personal equipment.

The king salmon can get quite large, and you may be catching them in very powerful rivers, especially if you go out to Kodiak Island. I've heard of a guy catching them on a 5-weight, but for a more conventional approach, I would say you need at least a 9-weight. You will cast big, weighted flies, heavy lines, and you will want long casts. Also, if you do hook a king, he will run downstream with no respect for you at all. A big rod may be the only chance you have for stopping him.

You can use this rod for the other salmon also, but they are not so tough. You should see a lot of sockeyes, especially at the Gorge. These fish are 5 to 10 pounds. A 6- or 7-weight will work pretty well for these fish.

The trout are big, but they are just trout. A 5-weight is my all-around favorite trout rod. It will be perfect for tackling the Copper River, which I thought was one of the finest trout rivers I have ever seen.

Also, bring a fun, light rod. The sight fishing for grayling is an amazing experience, and these fish are not too big. They also take minute dry flies and nymphs. I have a fantastic 5-piece 3-weight Winston that had its best day ever grayling fishing in Alaska. Indulge!

As far as reels go, use the same reels you would normally use for the trout and grayling, but be prepared for the salmon. A heavy Chinook could turn its tail on you, and have you running downstream for a mile. He could empty your reel like a bonefish. Have a reel with 200 yards of good backing for the King salmon.

LINES AND LEADERS

Use a double-tapered floating line for the trout, as it will give you more line control. For everything else, you will want a weight-forward floater line. To fish for the salmon, you will just want to make long casts and let the fly slowly swing around before you strip it back in. It can get very tiring, so you don't want to do more work than is necessary, and you will want to punch out a lot of distance easily. In terms of the depths of the lines, I find that salmon usually do not go too deep: even when they are at sea, they stay near the surface. A floating line

ABOVE: *The grayling is best known for its beautiful dorsal fin, which looks like a long sea fan running down much of its back. These fish are salmonids and are related to trout. They feed in the same water and take to the same flies as trout. Many of them don't get very large, but their bodies are very strong, and they put up a formidable fight.*

PREVIOUS PAGE: *The powerful upper gorge on the Newhalen River. Fish rest for weeks before struggling up these waters. The roar is so loud in places it is difficult to hear one another. Occasionally, a fisherman will see the tiny red helmet of a daring kayaker coming down these freezing rapids. The Rainbow King Lodge has almost exclusive access to these waters, and it would be easy to catch anywhere up to 50 salmon – if one was inclined to do so – in a day spent below the gorge where the salmon are resting.*

will work well in most situations. However, on Kodiak Island we fished one river in particular that had a deep, fast current. Here, we used a number 3 fast-sinking line to get down just a couple of feet beneath the surface.

A good strong leader, and plenty of backing, is a must with the salmon, especially the larger ones. The fish are heavy, and the currents can be strong, so don't taper down to anything less than 15 pounds with the Kings; 10 pounds is fine for all the others. The backing is important here. When you are salmon fishing in the Pacific, you will often foul hook your fish. The salmon stack up in huge schools beneath falls, and when the hook drags through, it often catches a dorsal or a tail fin. When this happens, you have very little control over the fish. It may run into a big current and empty your reel in no time, so make sure you have plenty of 20- to 30-pound backing.

THE FLY BOX

The trout and grayling will take your basic box of trout flies. Later in the season, hatches begin to take wing, so it is good to have plenty of dry flies. There are a good many mayfly patterns up there. The trout also love to spend the whole summer eating the remains of the dying salmon. The pink flesh floats downstream in droves, and the trout are waiting. A popular trout fly here is called Cotton Candy. It is a pink ball of wool tied to a hook that looks like loose fish flesh, and it works quite well.

You will be fishing the Copper river for sure, if you are after good rainbows. Fred is the local expert here. He has a lodge down in Chile, and works in Alaska during our summer out of sheer love of the sport. He has designed a system of fishing for rainbows with salmon egg patterns. He puts a bare hook on the end of your line. About 10 inches up from the hook, he stops a hand-painted salmon egg pattern on the line. The fish will take readily. You set the hook by yanking the egg out of its mouth and replacing it with the hook at the end of the line. It is very effective, and fun to try this new method. You are in excellent hands with Fred.

The salmon will also take salmon egg patterns. Many people fish for Chinooks with salmon eggs. The fish propagate their own genetic strain by eating up other salmon eggs. But in terms of fly patterns, you are just trying to annoy them into taking. The patterns we used were mostly Glo-bugs; you can also bring some Alaskabou, Christmas Tree, and Green Lantern Flies. The lodge has everything you need if you can't find these readily.

ESSENTIAL KIT

Multiple layers of clothing are probably more important here than anywhere else. Depending on where you will be fishing, it can get very cold in the mornings, and sweltering hot in the afternoons. Also, don't be surprised if you get some thunderstorms. Be ready to wrap up with a warm, waterproof wading jacket on the outside. You can shed layers as the day goes on.

The mosquitoes and midges are said to be very bad here. Personally, I have never seen a mosquito in Alaska, but I trust other people's stories. After a rain shower, the clouds of midges can get pretty thick. Some protection is advisable.

As far as waders are concerned, the water is extremely cold up here. It is mostly glacial runoff, so if you use Gore-Tex, try and wear some sweat pants underneath, or make sure they're lined. Alternatively, wear neoprene, which should keep you warm enough.

Finally, as always, bring a camera. The views are absolutely breathtaking in this part of the world. You will want some way to capture everything you see.

BELOW: *Kodiak Island is filled with miles of beautiful salmon rivers both large and small. Here, Amanda Creek shows that a very small body of water can still hold large numbers of salmon, in this case sockeyes. They race through the fast parts and rest in deeper, slower pools before making another run on the way up to their spawning grounds.*

ABOVE: *Memories of an arctic grayling, caught on a dry fly in water as pure and clear as this, are burned forever into the mind of anyone who has fished the Kijik River. There aren't many trout nor any salmon: it is a river almost exclusively inhabited by the grayling – a fish that can only live in the finest water on Earth. Places like this will always fill the memory and call a fly-fisherman from thousands of miles away.*

CONSERVATION WATCH

Although the salmon fishing in Alaska is currently quite strong, it is in danger of falling prey to the same forces that are endangering salmon fishing in other regions of the Pacific Northwest.

As I write, the single most destructive environmental problem affecting the salmon is occurring on the Columbia and Snake Rivers in Washington, Oregon, and Idaho. The situation has devastated the Pacific salmon stocks in those rivers, and can also adversely affect the Alaskan salmon fishery.

Years ago, when Lewis and Clark canoed down the Columbia River on their voyage of discovery, they could spear fish with ease as they passed. An estimated 10 to 15 million fish would swim up the Columbia and its tributaries. Last year, only some 3000 salmon made it through the dams. It is these dams that year after year take an increasing percentage of the schools.

In 1986, all coho salmon on the rivers were declared extinct. Several years later, both the sockeye and Chinook salmon were declared threatened. Today, they are listed as endangered under the Endangered Species Act and may become extinct by the bi-centennial of Lewis and Clark's triumphant journey. The steelhead rainbow trout are now threatened with extinction on the Columbia and Snake as well. The Snake River is the largest tributary of the Columbia. They are both beautiful and formidable rivers, which have been centerpieces of the country since its first discovery by Lewis and Clark, and for thousands of years before that by the indigenous peoples who lived there.

Both of these rivers make very rapid descents from the heights of the Rocky Mountains and eventually empty into the Pacific Ocean. Because of the energy produced by these rivers, there have been eight dams constructed that stand between the Pacific Ocean and the salmon's spawning grounds. These dams were built and run by the Army Corps of Engineers, and owned by the Federal Columbia River Power System. The electricity from these dams is sold by the Bonneville Power Administration. For years, scientists and political activists have lobbied strongly for the removal of four dams on the lower Snake River. These dams are responsible for the devastating effects on smolts trying to leave the river and make their run to the ocean. By blocking up the water and making the rivers a slow moving stream with several large reservoirs, the small smelt are under tremendous danger of predators and unnatural river situations.

In 1998, the Idaho Department of Fish and Game declared after extensive research that the four dams on the lower Snake River were the primary cause of the massive depletions of all five species of salmon and the steelhead trout. They concluded that by removing only the earthen portion of the dams that a normal river habitat would be restored and would guarantee an 80 per cent chance of salmon restoration over the next 50 years for the salmon who have not already become extinct. On March 16, 1999, a letter signed by 206 scientists was sent to President Clinton, concluding: "The weight of scientific evidence clearly shows that wild Snake River salmon and steelhead runs cannot be recovered under existing river conditions." In order to avoid their extinction, the removal of the earthen portions of the four Snake River Dams is a priority.

The President's administration decided to hold off until December 1999 to make a decision. At that time, they concluded there was not enough scientific evidence to warrant removal of the dams. However, it has become overwhelmingly obvious that these salmon will be extinct in a matter of years if action is not taken. Currently, less than one half of one percent of all smolts will mature into an adult that can spawn. For every 200 fish born, less than one fish will ever return. These conditions are finalizing the extinction of these runs of fish and must be stopped.

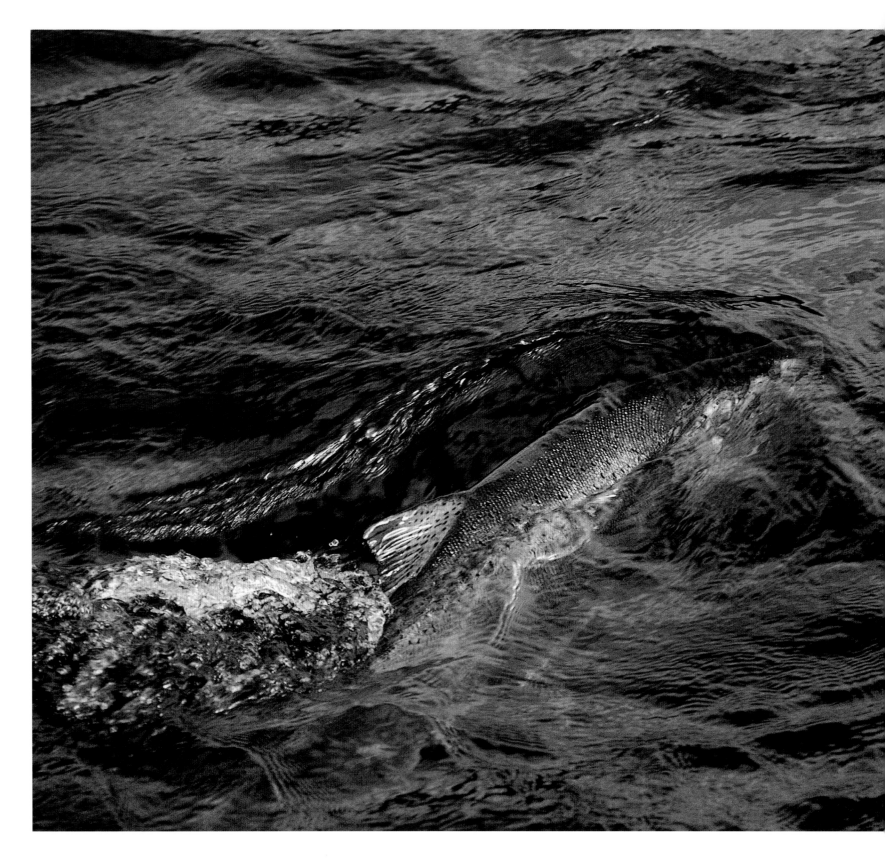

ABOVE: *Most of the Chinook salmon, like this one hooked on Kodiak Island in the Karluk River, are so large they break off before they get this close. These were the first king salmon runs of the year to come in, still silver from the ocean. This means they are strong and can put up one of fly-fishing's greatest fights. They will leap, thrash their heads, and head for the strongest currents to rid their mouths of the hook.*

RIGHT: *Once on the verge of extinction, the Bald Eagle – the symbol of America's freedom – lives in strong numbers in Alaska. One day we saw one dive straight into the water from more than 100 feet in the air. After several seconds underwater, the bird came back up but was unable to fly. Using its wings to breaststroke to the bank, it hopped out with a 40-50 lb king salmon in its claws. He spent the afternoon eating it while we fished much less effectively from the banks.*

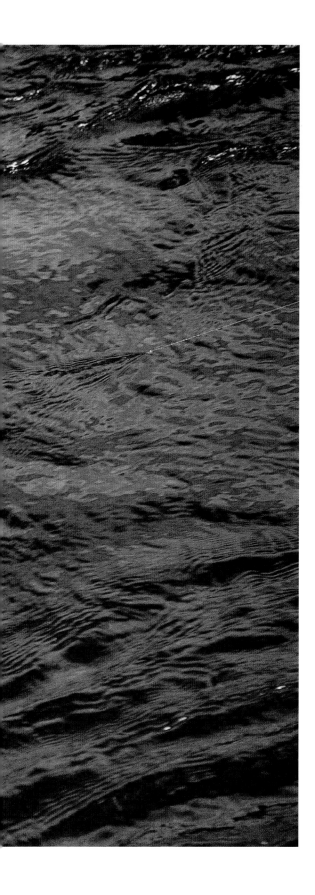

With these fish gone, unanswered demand could affect the species of fish in Alaska as well. As there is a need for salmon from the Pacific, with the depletion of the Columbia River salmon, the next target will be the fish migrating to and from Alaska. It would be a shame if within only 250 years of settling this country, we destroy a history of fish dating back thousands of years.

If this situation is not resolved by the time of the publication of this book, you can get involved through the following organizations. In addition, if these dams are removed, you can still monitor and join the fight that will take decades to restore the salmon through these same agencies.

FOLLOWING PAGES: *A glacier lake in Katmai National Park doesn't hold fish, but is still a beautiful site. The water is so cold it is pure blue in some places. Many of these glaciers have been frozen solid for thousands of years. In the summer, parts of them melt off and fill the rivers with frigid* *water. Landing in these lakes in a bush plane is a job for only the most experienced bush pilots in Alaska.*

Save our Wild Salmon Coalition 975 John Street #204 Seattle WA 98109 Tel: 206-622-2904 website: www.removedams.org

American Rivers 150 Nickerson Street #311 Seattle WA 98109 Tel: 206-213-0330

The Alaskan Department of Fish and Game PO Box 25526 Juneau AK 99802 Tel: 907-465-4180

GLOBE-TROTTER'S
GAZETTEER

Every dedicated fisherman knows that there is so much more to fishing than just fishing. After a trip around the world to the finest fly fishing destinations in existence, the truth of this is even clearer to me. We travelled to every inhabited continent on Earth in search of the ultimate in fly fishing, and yet one of the greatest joys of each new place was meeting new people and discovering a new culture. In this Gazetteer , as well as explaining the best time of year at which to visit the countries we fished, I have given an outline of the lodges and hotels that hosted us on our trip, and the people who made us so welcome. Each hotel, each lodge, has its own charm, but I have no hesitation in recommending them all enthusiastically. They were all incredibly friendly, and they looked after us wonderfully. Of course, there are many other destinations in the world, but I promise that the ones listed here made for the fly-fishing trip of a lifetime.

BOTSWANA

WHEN TO GO

Like many things in this part of the world, the fishing seasons are governed heavily by the weather. Almost all of the Okavango Delta is fed by the monsoon rains, which fall in the highlands and drain out through the Delta to the Kalahari Desert.

From December through March, the rains come down by the bucket load. The waters rise and begin to flood south. During the months of March–May, the water levels are very high. This is when we went, and we caught plenty of fish, but there could have been many more.

In the months from August–October, the water levels fall greatly during the dry season. In the northern half of the Delta, this reveals numerous islands and streams emerging from the permanent swamp. In the south, the plains dry up and leave behind only a few small streams.

During these dry months, the Okavango Delta is a good place to be for the angler. The barbel (known in the United States as a type of catfish) begin to congregate and make huge runs up the river. These fish enter the moss along the banks and the papyrus mazes to feed upon the smaller fish hiding. Always close behind is the tiger fish ready to feed upon the minnows running from the barbel. This is the season to catch both barbel and really large tiger fish.

The tiger fishing tends to be prolific right through the beginning of the monsoon season. Only in the spring does it fall off a bit, but there are still fish to catch. A phone call to the camp is the best way to find out how the season is progressing.

WHERE TO STAY

There are several lodges from which you can fish on the Delta, but I would recommend **Nxamaseri Lodge** (pronounced NAH-mah-sari). It is the quintessential Botswana fly-fishing lodge. It has recently been taken over by new owners who are making it more affordable for the international fly-fisherman and game watcher.

The founder of the lodge was P. J. Bestelink. He was first based there in the 60s, and it is said that he was one of the first people to catch a tiger fish on a fly. He still lives in Botswana and comes to the lodge from time to time. His mark remains there still.

The lodge is set right on the banks of a slow canal on the Okavango Delta. You arrive at the nearby landing strip by plane and take boats from

there to the dock. From the dock you are led into a beautiful area where guests enjoy outdoor fires during much of the fishing season. There is an old-fashioned circular bar, with mounts of large tiger fish on the wall, and palm leaves woven into the ceiling.

The accommodation is very good. Each room is actually its own little hut with private bathrooms and private patios overlooking the water. It could not be more African. There are large lizards and even some monkeys in the trees. The beds are draped in old-fashioned mosquito netting, and lanterns light your room at night. Unfortunately, I was alone when I went there, but it is an incredibly romantic place.

Dinner each night is served at the dining table in the bar, where they provide chicken and lamb, African salads, fish, and almost everything else. There are plenty of bottles of hot sauce on the table, and a lot of cold drinks coming from the bar. It is a very festive atmosphere.

At night some of the guys have been known to go out and spot "crocs" from the boats. It is quite a sight; I will just leave it at that. Nxamaseri was one of the best memories I have of the whole trip.

The contact details are:

Nxamaseri Camp
Private Bag 23
Maun, Botswana
Tel: +267 66 1671
Fax: +267 66 1672

SOUTH AFRICA

WHEN TO GO

Everyone in and around Lydenberg prefers the fishing around the time of the South African autumn. This is from about April to May. Although you can fish throughout the year, the summers can get quite warm especially down below at Highland run, and the fish are then sluggish.

The autumn produces a tremendous amount of late season mayfly hatches that bring the trout out of their warm weather blues. Spinners floating in droves down the river fatten the fish up, and help them take to the fly easily.

Through their winter and spring the fishing continues to be quite good, but it can snow a good deal on Mount Anderson in the winter. The springtime, from September to October, also produces a good many hatches of mayflies and terrestrials. In addition, many of the minnows and tadpoles are coming out of their eggs, which the trout are aggressively feeding on throughout the season. Call Mala-Mala Game Reserves to discuss the best time to go.

WHERE TO STAY

I could only recommend one lodge in which to stay if you are planning on fly-fishing. **Mount Anderson Ranch** is located in Lydenburg, just a three-hour drive east of Johannesburg. There, we were lucky enough to be hosted by the owners of the famous Rattray Game Reserves, the most famous game reserves in South Africa.

If you have ever been to Mala Mala or one of their other reserves, you will know it is a strong statement to say that the lodge at Mount Anderson is a bit more luxurious than the others. It is the personal vacation home for the Rattray family from time to time, and is a true monument to the ideal South African country home.

When you arrive, you must drive up an 8-mile driveway before you see anything but brush and the remnants of the steaming hot South

African countryside. Above 3,000 feet, the fields become lush and sprawling, disappearing into the distance. Massive rock formations jut high above you as you reach the peaks of some of the ridges. The road eventually winds up to the top, and then turns to descend into a valley on the other side of a ridge, where the house in nestled quietly into a wide crevasse of rocks.

This is the kind of place anyone would want to have if they could. The rooms are large and comfortable. There is both a formal dining room and a patio with a walk-in grille for parties. Then, just beneath the patio is a series of weirs running down the valley, each well stocked with trout ready to take flies any time of the day. There is a large living room with several seating areas scattered tastefully throughout. Finally, at the end of the evening, you can retire to the billiard room for a game on their full-size snooker table. Adjacent to this is a room that I could only call the cognac-drinking room. Shadow boxes and old paintings adorn the walls, and we never wanted to leave.

Surrounding the house here is the 20,000-acre game reserve. Looking in all directions, all you can see is your own private wildlife sanctuary with a full panorama of wildebeest, 11 different species of antelope, birds, big cats, hogs, and, most importantly, fish.

If ever it is too cold, or some people in your party just do not feel like fishing, you can simply stay at home, or get into the Land Rovers and spend hours watching Africa unfold before your eyes. It is truly one of the most beautiful places in the world.

There is only room for one party at a time. The lodge can only fit 10-12 people at the most. So, if you are looking for a place to quietly take your family away from the world for a week or two, you could not dream up a place more perfect than the Mount Anderson Ranch.

David Evans is a director of the Rattray Game Reserves, and the manager of the Mount Anderson Ranch.
The contact details are:
Mount Anderson Ranch Booking Office
Mala Mala & Mashatu Game Reserves
Private Bag X284, Hillcrest
3650 Kwazulu-Natal, South Africa
Tel: +27 31 765 2900
Fax: +27 31 765 3365
Email: reservations@malamala.com
Web: www.malamala.com

ARGENTINA

WHEN TO GO

It is always important to remember that, being in the southern hemisphere, Argentina's seasons are the opposite of those in the US. When our seasons start to close down, theirs are just getting started. This is why a lot of lodge operators in North America, especially Canada and Alaska, have second lodges down in South America.

Air/water temperatures and water volume in the rivers affect the fishing seasons most. The early season in Chubut, Patagonia, opens around November 15, and goes through April 15. The season ends thereabouts, as most of the salmonoids will begin to spawn. Fishing is closed during the spawning seasons to allow the fish to recuperate and reproduce.

The fishing in Argentina is so good, it is not overly important when you go – you are bound to catch a great many fish. We arrived late in the season, and still caught a plethora of nice fish every day. It is more

important to take into account your personal preferences, as each season has different characteristics.

October through December – their spring – is when the season gets started. These months are marked by water run-off from the snow, and cool temperatures. The rivers will be higher, and some of the smaller streams will be more fishable, than later in the year when the water levels begin to come down. In the late season, March to May, the water levels will fall a great deal, as the snow is no longer melting, and the water temperatures will rise. The downside to this is that warmer water can make fish sluggish, and some of the smaller streams may not have enough water to fish. However, the bigger streams will be low enough for nice wading, and the colors in the trees make for absolutely beautiful scenery.

Whichever way you look at it, both the early and late seasons have pluses and minuses. This is Argentina, and any time during the season will provide outstanding fishing opportunities. The dry flies begin their famous hatches in January and go through to March, which makes for excellent mayfly fishing. If you pick somewhere in the middle of the season you could not go wrong. If you're still worried, call O'Farrell's Lodge and ask what they recommend. They live there all year round and will know what the conditions are like.

WHERE TO STAY

There are a great many fly-fishing lodges throughout Argentina, but I would only recommend one. **O'Farrell's Trevelin Lodge** could not have been a nicer place to stay.

Martin O'Farrell owns the lodge. a very energetic and very charismatic man, who rarely stops moving, whether it is around town or around Argentina. Almost his entire family helps him run the lodge. His brother-in-law, John Roberts, is the manager, and his delightful parents, Eleanor and Hubert keep you feeling right at home in the evenings, and at dinner.

The dinners, and the food in general, need a special mention. Martin's brother, Pablo, is the cook. We were absolutely amazed at the elegance and quality of the meals we received so far out in the middle of nowhere. He will cook amazing steaks over charcoal; he has an enormous pizza oven in which he cooks his famous Argentine Pizza, and breakfasts and lunch will not be bettered at any lodge in the world. His dishes are incredibly diverse and could easily be served in any top restaurant in New York. He is a young man, and rumor had it while we were there that there was some competition amongst the local ladies for his food and companionship. Once you try his pizza, you'll understand.

The lodge itself is very comfortable. There are five rooms, and these can accommodate parties of 12 or more if necessary. It feels like an old log house, but very comfortable. It is in the middle of a wide valley in the Andes Mountains. From any window in the house, you can see snow-covered peaks, and jagged cliffs rising above you. The lodge itself is not right on a river. However, it is situated in a perfectly central location to provide access to every great river in the region – most notably the Rio Grande and the Rio Rivadavia. If you are going to Patagonia, this place will really show you what it is all about.

The contact details are:

O'Farrell's Trevelin Lodge
P.O. Box 7, (9203) Trevelin
Chubut-Patagonia
Argentina
Tel: +54 2945 480324
or +54 2945 480365
Email: martin@trevelin.com
ofarrell@netesquel.com.ar
Web:www.trevelin.com

NEW ZEALAND

SOUTH ISLAND – WHEN TO GO

As in Argentina, remember that the seasons in New Zealand are the exact opposite of ours, as these islands are also in the southern hemisphere. In general, the season opens around the 1st of October, and closes around the late part of April, depending on where you are in the country.

The joy of catching these trout is doing it with a dry fly. November is when the dry flies really start to hatch in numbers. By January and February, the dry fly fishing is considered excellent, before tapering off toward the end of the season

March is really the last decent dry fly month, although you will continue to use them throughout the season to some degree. Each part of the season has its ups and downs, but the couple of months after Christmas are probably the best.

Our guide, David Pike, was the best guide I have ever had. He used to camp in the woods along these backcountry streams and fish all summer. He told me that every 5–6 years the beechnuts shed their nuts. They lie all over the forest bottom, and the mice eat them up. When they start fermenting, the mice continue to eat them, but it makes them drunk, and they fall into the rivers in great numbers. The trout eat them, and grow to enormous sizes, and take to mouse patterns. I do not know when it will happen next, but if you call him through the lodge, he may tell you.

SOUTH ISLAND – WHERE TO STAY

I could not recommend a better place to go for a wonderful fishing experience than the **Motueka River Lodge**, run by Mick and Fiona Mason. The Motueka River runs right past the front yard – just a five-minute walk down the drive. And as you come up, you are surrounded by Mick's private wine orchards.

The first thing I must say about this fantastic find is that Fiona may be the best cook we found anywhere in the world. Every night we were amazed at the quality of the food. You could not be fed better, no matter where you went.

The accommodation is very comfortable. There are several large rooms with king-size beds and private bathrooms. The view from each room is beautiful. In the evenings, I would stroll out on the back deck, and if I looked up the hillside I would see the beautiful silhouette of a red stag coming down the mountain. There are vines growing up the wooden posts on the deck, and you could easily drift away thinking that you were in Provence.

We loved everything about this part of the trip. Nothing could have been better. I still have dreams about the helicopters arriving in the morning and landing on the front yard beside the orchards. I would rush to get my bacon finished and be waiting in the front seat before anyone else had shown up.

The contact details are:

Motueka River Lodge
P.O. Box 238, Motueka
New Zealand
Tel: +64 3 526 8868
Fax: +64 3 526 8669
Email: enquiries@motuekalodge.co.nz
Web: www.motuekalodge.co.nz

NORTH ISLAND – WHEN TO GO

The good thing about the Turangi area is that parts of New Zealand stay open to fishing all year. Even in the southern winter, July and August, there is excellent river fishing in Tongariro and Tauranga-Taupo. But aside from that difference, most things are the same as in the South Island.

The season opens for the most part in October, but many of the fish will still be in the lakes. The fishing at the estuaries to the rivers can prove quite productive if you know what "rips" to cast over. As this is usually top secret information, become friends with a local guide.

The dry flies start to hatch around November in the mountain streams and get progressively better right through to March, when the hatch activity starts to die off. However, as this activity is dying off, you are really starting to get large numbers of the spawning rainbows coming up the Tongariro and the Tauranga-Taupo. This is the most exciting of all fishing, as these fish can get extremely large and brimfull with that spawning determination.

NORTH ISLAND – WHERE TO STAY

The lodge we stayed in is one of the great New Zealand fishing lodges. **Tongariro River Lodge** is run by a man named Tony Hayes. Situated

right along the Tongariro River, it is in a perfect spot for a lodge. The town of Turangi has a sign when you enter that says, "*Turangi: The Trout Fishing Capital of the World.*"

The lodge itself is a very large series of log cabins. The whole place is capable of hosting a good-size business convention. There is a large central meeting area with dining room, game room, and a very comfortable area to sit by the fire and drink Scotch. The food is excellent, and supplemented by an excellent wine list. Many of the wines are from New Zealand and Australia, which have become world-class wine regions.

It is also very exciting in the morning as the helicopters are coming in and out to pick people up for the day and transport them deep into the backcountry. The wind hits your face as they land, and you really wake up and feel like a commando being sent away on a special mission.

Tony Hayes has created an incredible sanctuary here, where you go in and feel as though there is no one else around. You are in a relatively populated area, but you would never know it, and each cabin seems rather isolated, even though you can play tennis here, or come with 30 of your friends. We had a great stay.

There is such a wide variety of fishing at this lodge. Between the spawning rainbows, and the helicopter flyouts, you can find superb fishing in beautiful waters all year round. Just call the lodge to discuss exactly what you would like to do.

The contact details are:
Tongariro Lodge
P.O. Box 278
Turangi
New Zealand
Tel: +64 7 386 7946
Fax: +64 7 386 8860
Email: trout@reap.org.nz
Web: www.tongarirolodge.co.nz

BHUTAN

WHEN TO GO

The fishing up in the Himalayas is very much dependent on the forces of nature. One day, an absolutely crystal clear river we were fishing turned the deep color of red Georgia clay in about five seconds due to a landslide further upstream.

After the end of the winter, there is a tremendous amount of runoff due to the milder temperatures. Once that ends, the fishing season begins in about April and continues through May or June. The monsoon season starts in June and goes on through the summer. This brings a tremendous amount of rain, and poor fishing and travel conditions. The roads become very muddy and dangerous. In the fall, the fishing can be quite productive. By September, the rains have usually ceased, and the next few months can be very prolific until the winter snows blanket the Himalayas.

I would choose to go in the spring. Unlike Nepal or Tibet, Bhutan is an incredibly lush country with extensive areas of forest. Hydrangeas can be found everywhere, and when the country is in bloom, it is a sight one will never forget.

WHERE TO STAY

In terms of guiding and lodging, there is only one group to go with, but they are extremely good. Ugyen Rinzin runs **Yangphel Tours and Travels**. He can custom design any type of trip you want to take. It can be all fly-fishing or some fishing, some kayaking, some hiking. Bhutan is like an enormous (very distinguished) playground with so much to do.

As a fisherman, you will be very well taken care of. You will arrive on Druk Air, which is the Royal airline, into Paro on the far western end of the country. From there you will continuously work your way in a zigzag line to the west. Thimphu, Bumthang, Gangtey, and Punakha will all be stops along your journey.

In some valleys, there were farmers who would walk throughout the night with bells ringing to try to keep the wild boar out of their crops. They erect sheds out in the fields to sleep in. One night, I actually went out bow hunting with little bamboo arrows and poison but had no luck. Every place has its own character, completely different from any other.

Bhutan is by no means your normal or average fly-fishing destination, but you will always be perfectly comfortable and well taken care of by the people there. The accommodations are very nice, and the oriental food is the "real deal."

Contact Ugyen directly to talk about setting up a customized trip.

The contact details are:
Yangphel Tours and Travels
P.O. Box 236
Thimphu
Kingdom of Bhutan
Tel: +975 2 323293
Fax: +975 2 322897
Email: infos@yangphel.com.bt

IRELAND

WHEN TO GO

The salmon here will usually begin to saturate the rivers from February to June. These spring run salmon can weigh anywhere between 10 and 20lbs. "Springers" can be the greatest trophies. However, if you make your reservations too early, you may find that the fish are still waiting to come in. It is best to check with your lodge and ask when the spring runs typically get started.

The grilse (a salmon that returns to the river after only one year at sea) and summer salmon usually arrive from late May onwards. The largest peak runs are in June and early July. The grilse are between 3 and 10lbs but are young and will give you a stronger fight than you may imagine.

Toward the end of the season, there will be more fish in the rivers. However, they tend to be a bit more sluggish than the earlier fish straight from the ocean. They are not quite so strong, and their colors don't shine so brightly. But, you may catch more. Talk to your hosts and inquire about when the best time of the year is.

WHERE TO STAY

We stayed in three places when we visited Ireland, the first of which was the most up-market and luxurious. **Ballynahinch** is in the central western county of Galway, in the town of Ballynahinch. Our second stop was the Drowes fishery in the far northern town of Kenlough. We were treated like family in the small, but comfortable **Neely's Bed and Breakfast**. This was a last minute arrangement, as we heard reports that fish were being landed in the north. The Irish attitude is, "Well if they're up there now, they've got to come here next. Let's have a drink in the meantime." We on the other hand were a little less sure; so we headed north. Our final stop was in the town of Leenane, where we were hosted by Peter Mantle at the **Delphi Lodge**. Delphi was once the country estate of the Count of Sligo, and later home to Mountbatten before his grisly demise at the hands of the Irish Republican Army.

Ballynahinch

Ballynahinch is the ultimate prototype of an extremely elegant getaway for country living and sport. The castle sits atop 13,000 acres of useable land for pheasant drives, woodcock hunting, and angling beats. Every morning when we'd wake, we were met in the breakfast room by a finely dressed mix of anglers and hunters. In the next room over, our ghillies would meet to set their sails straight with a little dram of this or that.

We would set up on a stretch of water that was set aside as our beat for the day. By anyone's standards, these beats are beautiful. There is a tremendously potent and formidable feeling in your blood standing beside a relatively small country chalk-stream when beneath you is a run of salmon containing fish anywhere up to 30lbs or more.

As the river winds through the Ballynahinch valley, large lakes have formed, and beside these you can find some of the most beautiful country houses you could imagine. The calm mirror-like water may have a large boulder in the middle as the only thing to break the magnificent reflection of the landscape.

Perhaps the most memorable beat we had was on the last day, when we had the beat in front of the castle all to ourselves. Spey casting in full view of this dramatic, old castle reminded me how much I love to travel and fish. The sun was out, and the salmon were sluggish, so we didn't have any luck. But, I still walked home with a smile, and I wish to God I could be there now.

The contact details are:

Ballynahinch Castle
Recess
Connemara
County Galway
Ireland
Tel: +353 95 31006
Fax: +353 95 31085
Email: bhinch@iol.ie
Web: www.commerce.ie/ballynahinch/

Drowes Fishery

We came to the Drowes fishery in Kenlough because our ghillie informed us there was a tremendous problem with sea lice in the south. However, a visiting expert who owns the French magazine *Saumon Atlantique* told me that the sea lice don't really kill the salmon, they only cause problems for the sea trout. Then, our ghillie's story changed. Suddenly, El Niño was the cause of the extreme heat keeping the fish from running. Whatever the reason, we were not catching anything at Ballynahinch, and we had good reports about the Drowes.

The Drowes fishery, although much simpler and humbler than anything else we saw, was easily my favorite stop in all of Ireland. We stayed at the home of the Neelys, **Neely's Bed and Breakfast**, one of the many B&B's in this area in which you can stay. You can find them by contacting Bill Likely in the Drowes Fishery office in Laureen Park.

The Drowes River was an incredible fishing experience. Again, not many salmon were caught in 1998, but if you were going to catch them, this was where they would be. Aside from the fish, the collection of scenery, characters, and laughs was unbeatable.

Bill Likely, a funny and mischievous man who liked making funny faces at me, is the warden of the river and will always be waiting for you in the office in Laureen Park. He will get you your licence and get you started on where to go on the four-mile stretch of water flowing down to the sea.

Starting at Four Heads Bridge (named after the four bronze heads of the monks who wrote the first complete history of Ireland), there was a cast of quintessential characters. Beside the bridge sat four old men who never seemed to move. They sat with their pipes and discussed the rest of us, contemplated the river, and stood up to stretch every now and then.

The river itself was one of the finest fishing experiences I have ever had. Starting from the Drowes Lake at the top, the river is a slow winding chalk stream with deep, dark pools that can hold very large salmon. As it winds down the valley, the river steepens a bit and becomes more of a freestone stream with protruding rocks and mild rapids. The salmon can be found just about anywhere, as they are not resting in any particular feeding stations but traveling from the bottom to the top and resting in pools from time to time to store up energy for their blistering runs.

I caught my first Atlantic salmon in the Sea Pool, and it was the most beautiful fish I have ever seen. It took me at least a thousand casts. I have never worked harder for a fish. I have also never felt so well rewarded.

Delphi Lodge

Delphi is another fantastic spot that I highly recommend. Situated in Leenane, which is in the County Mayo region, Delphi is surrounded by the highest mountains in the Connacht Mountain range. Through the valley winds the Delphi River system, which forms four large lakes where the salmon rest during the season, and five miles of fishable river where the salmon make their runs.

Peter Mantle is the owner of the Delphi Lodge and he has the wit and humor to handle a household of needy fly-fisherman in want of flies, rods, and some of the best food we had on the entire trip. He is also known throughout the world for the work he has done to rejuvenate the salmon fishery at Delphi. He takes particular interest in the environment, and makes himself an active player in the fight to save the species.

The fishing at Delphi was very well run. Everyone we talked to in Ireland was always talking about sea lice and about commercial fisherman who diseased and decimated the fish. But no one ever talked about doing anything about it. Well, Peter does more than complain; he lobbies, and he was actually involved in taking a commercial fishery to court while we were there. He is a very funny man, but takes conservation very seriously. You can be sure the ecosystem along the Delphi is in very good hands.

One day, I caught the largest salmon of the week here and, as tradition dictates, I had to sit at the head of the long, elegant dining table where all the guests come to eat. Everyone sits and discusses the day, and the scene truly resembles a presidential state dinner. Waitresses serve game and fish, the sommelier takes the wine order, and we all applaud the cook at the end of the feast. This was a true Irish country treat.

The contact details are:

Delphi Lodge
Leenane
County Galway
Ireland
Tel: +353 95 42222
Fax: +353 95 42296
Email: info@delphilodge.ie
Web: www.delphilodge.ie

SCOTLAND

WHEN TO GO

The season is open by February, but the fishing never really starts up for another few weeks, or even months. Each season has its own character, and therefore things to consider before deciding when to go.

The first consideration is that all of the water you will be fishing is private, and you will be assigned a beat each day. This beat will be yours exclusively, but you cannot leave it. Some of these beats are booked years in advance. People are religious about their favorite beats and rivers in Scotland, so make sure you reserve your place early.

The first run of fish is in the spring. They start coming up in February and continue through March, April, and May. By most standards, these salmon are considered the true trophies. They are fresh out of the ocean, shining silver, and have a few sea lice on them. The sea lice are an indication that they have been in fresh water less than 48 hours, because after that the lice fall off.

Some fishermen are so insistent that these "springers" are the only real fish to catch that they will only fish in the springtime. These are beautiful and very strong fish, but they are also very scarce and difficult to catch. Given the choice, anyone would choose a nice spring run salmon over an

older fish later in the season, but be ready for a lot of hard work, and go as late in the spring as you can. We were there in March and still caught a few, but it was only one a day, if any at all.

The other option for you is to go in the summer and fall, up until October. This is probably when most fish are taken. The rivers have had an entire summer for the fish to come up from the ocean to spawn. There are thousands of them in the river at this point, but catching them is still quite difficult, as they are not interested in eating. There will be far more takes to your fly, but the quality of the fish will not be as great. Later in the season, the fish are more tired than when they first came up out of the ocean. Their color has died off a bit, and they will not fight as hard.

So there are serious pluses and minuses to each season. Personally, I would say be a purist and go for the springers. But, go in the late spring, when you have a fighting chance of getting a couple in a day.

WHERE TO STAY

The thing I found so nice about traveling through Scotland is that even if you do not stay in one of the premier fishing lodges or country houses, many of the basic bed and breakfasts are very distinguished. Small innkeepers very often put flowers in all the rooms, the country food is good, and everyone here is quite friendly. However, there were a couple of places we stayed that were worthy of considerable mention.

The Forss House

This hotel is run by Jamie MacGregor, whom you would definitely call a good Scotsman. Not only is he from one of the oldest clans in Scotland, but he also plays the bagpipes. At a recent party held on the Thurso River to celebrate the fishing season, Jamie was seen playing the pipes at sunset as one of his colleagues fought a nice salmon to the net. He has every Scottish whisky in existence in his hotel, and guests congregate in the bar at night to talk about the day on the river. The rooms are enormous and plush, the food is absolutely outstanding, and the service couldn't be friendlier. There is not much more you could expect from a salmon lodge.

The nicest thing about this hotel is the setting. It is set apart from the main town, and is placed in a small wood at the bottom of a vast, windswept Highland landscape. Just out the front door is the Forss River, which has very nice numbers of salmon, and is privately held by the hotel for guests. The Falls Pool is one of the most productive in the area. And a one-mile walk along excellent fishing water brings you to a breathtaking estuary where the river cascades across several hundred yards of rocks and cliffs to finally empty into the sea.

Colonies of seals wait for the salmon in this estuary. The fishermen do not like them, but they are a beautiful sight to behold. The overall aura of staying in this hotel was magical and truly Scottish. I would recommend this hotel as one of the best, and certainly most enjoyable, in northern Scotland. Make sure to call Jamie before you go. He is an excellent fisherman, and you could not ask for a better host. His brother has another lodge and has access to the famous Naver and Borgie Rivers, so as well as being an excellent host, Jamie is a well respected man who can get you onto any of the neighboring river beats with just a little notice.

The contact details are:

The Forss Country House Hotel
Forss, near Thurso, Caithness
KW14 7XY Scotland
Tel: +44 1847 861201
Email: info@forsscountryhouse.co.uk
Web: www.forsscountryhouse.co.uk

The Ulbster Arms Hotel

This hotel, owned by Lord Thurso, is located right on the Thurso River. You can watch the water skirt by just outside the window. The Ulbster Arms is something of a centerpiece for the fishing community. At night, everyone comes in to sit at the bar and tell his or her fishing stories, and many of them are guests. The rooms are extremely nice, and usually filled with serious salmon fishermen, many of whom come year after year as a matter of tradition.

The warden of the river, Eddie McCarthy, is usually to be found in the hotel in the evening, filling the logbooks with figures from the day's catch. There is a very friendly and traditional feel to the place.

The restaurant and bar are the nicest in the town of Thurso. You can eat in the dining room, or in the pub. In both, you will be served food from a cook who specializes in international cuisine. The menu is carefully prepared to include everything from Scottish beef to Moroccan chicken and Cajun sausage. Their whisky selection is more limited than the Forss House, but most people here are locals just drinking beer and catching up on the news.

The contact details are:

The Ulbster Arms Hotel
Bridge Street, Halkirk
Caithness KW12 6XY
Scotland
Tel/Fax: +44 1847 831206
Email: info@ulbsterarms.co.uk
Web: www.ulbsterarms.co.uk

BAHAMAS

WHEN TO GO

The three factors that will affect your fishing the most in the Bahamas are wind, tides, and fish. The tides are always predictable by the moon. There are two low and two high tides a day. The locals will be able to tell you where the fish are… hopefully. So the most important consideration in choosing when to go is the wind – and the weather in general.

The fish are cruising the flats every day of the year. They never migrate. However, your ability to find them is very dependent upon the local

weather conditions. Without any sun, it is nearly impossible to see through the water and spot any fish. Then, if the wind is blowing, it can distort the surface of the water to the point where not only is it difficult to cast, but almost impossible to see any fish.

There are a couple of guidelines that you can follow to plan your trip. Planning anything in the Bahamas requires you to be a full-time weather watcher. Storms and wind, which can be more powerful here than anywhere on Earth, will obviously ruin a bonefishing trip.

The hurricane season starts in June and extends through till the winter. August and September are when experienced anglers and sailors really start to be wary. Strong low-pressure systems can build quickly into tropical storms and hurricanes, making for an entire blackout on the water. You have to get inside and stay put. This is probably the worst time to go, as you have a good chance of some storms.

The winter weather can be testy if a norther blows through, but then things generally begin to get a little more quiet, much to the relief of the locals. After the last norther, usually in May or so, the weather is ruled entirely by an easterly flow of maritime air. This is probably the best time of the year for bonefishing. The winds die down a bit, and clouds and storms are a little less common.

However, the weather in the Bahamas is extremely unpredictable. Squalls pop up all the time. You could be enjoying a bright blue sunshiny day when suddenly a 15-minute squall passes through, ruining visibility. Winds can jump to 30mph or more, and an inch of rainfall could come down in no time. These squalls usually pass in about 15 minutes, and you can watch them slowly meander their way around the islands all day.

So you can go any time of the year and have a great chance of catching fish, but late spring/early summer is probably the best bet on the weather.

WHERE TO STAY

When we went to the Bahamas, we went to the Islands of Andros. There are many respectable lodges on these islands, but one of the best is **Moxey's Guesthouse and Bonefishing Lodge**. The Moxey family has been in the fishing business since the first half of the century. In the early 1930s wealthy Americans began coming to the Bahamas on vacation. The most notable of these families was Andrew Mellon and his wife. They came consistently to Middle Bight, Andros, and hired bonefishing guides out of Moxeytown, thus founding the tradition of several generations of excellent fishing guides in the Moxey family.

Joel Moxey is currently the head of the clan, and he is in charge of the day-to-day operations of the lodge. He still guides, but if he is unavailable, there are several local guides who are also very capable. Our favorite was John Wayne. He has an ego to match his name, but is one of the most fun and talented guides we had on our trip. He will get you into some fish.

Like all lodges in the Bahamas, the accommodation is clean but very simple. The emphasis here is on the fishing and the bar. They have several skiffs on the beach to get you out to the flats whenever you need to go. At day's end, Lundi, the charismatic barkeeper, who can make anything you want, and even suggest some new Bahamian drinks of his own, heads the bar, and provides the jokes.

The food is traditional Bahamian fare. This includes the classic "conch fritters," grilled snapper, salads, ice tea, etc. They will also make you hamburgers or anything else that you want.

All of your creature comforts will be taken care of. The rooms have air conditioning, showers, comfortable beds, and plenty of room. Right out in front of the lodge is the beach where you load up the boats in the morning, and there are plenty of palm trees to relax under and contemplate the sunset. It is an excellent bonefishing lodge.

The contact details are:

Moxey's Guesthouse & Bonefish Lodge
Moxey Town, Mangrove Cay
Andros Island, The Bahamas
Tel: +242 369 0023 or +242 362 2186
Fax: +242 369 0726
Email: pax@bahamas.net.bs
Web: www.moxeybonefish.com

ALASKA

WHEN TO GO

Alaska is at very high latitudes and receives a good deal of snowfall during the winter that does not melt until the springtime comes around. This adds to the size of the glaciers in the mountains. The fishing season is completely dependent upon when the glaciers melt, and subsequently when the water levels rise and water temperatures begin to suit the salmon waiting in the estuaries. The seasons vary by as much as several weeks each season.

It would be possible to go into incredible depth about the factors affecting the fish, and why the fishing is better when it is, but if you want this kind of information, contact the Alaska Department of Fish and Game. Jon Lyman is the director.

However, in terms of a relatively accurate schedule of events, it is safe to make a bet that August is probably the best month to go to Illiamna and Kodiak Island for the full panorama of fish.

The king and sockeye salmon start making their runs in April and May respectively. They both end around August. The pink and coho salmon both begin around July and go through September and November respectively. The chum make a short run from June to August.

If you are interested in catching trophy rainbows, probably the best time to go would be in September. This is after they have spent the whole season feeding on salmon, and have reached enormous sizes. They are still in the rivers following the coho, and busy eating up any eggs that have drifted off the gravel beds. The grayling should also be outstanding this time of the year.

WHERE TO STAY

There are many lodges and outfitters you can fish with if you go to Alaska, but if you want to really *experience* Alaska, you have to do it right. **The Rainbow King Lodge** is one of the premier fly-fishing lodges in all of Alaska. If you look west of Anchorage on a map, you will find a sizeable lake named Lake Illiamna. The lodge is located in the town of Illiamna.

The lake is known by ichthyologists around the world to contain some of the largest rainbow trout in the world. Like all rainbows, they prefer lakes to rivers, but they always come up the rivers when the snow melts, in order to feed on the salmon eggs and to spawn. It is without a doubt one of the top three rainbow fisheries on Earth. And the very best of it is within easy access of the lodge.

The lodge has access to innumerable rivers and lakes, with outposts set up on about ten of their favorites. To reach the fishing at these inaccessible sites, you are transported in an Alaskan bush plane (Beavers and Otters with DeHavilland engines) in the morning, and this is an experience in itself. Flying over the mountains is an amazing way to wake up, and a wonderful

start to the day. Beneath you is one of the greatest landscapes in existence – snow-capped mountains, mirror lakes, bears, moose, and caribou, and you will not find another human in sight.

As you approach your landing sight on some remote lake or river, the pilot will usually sweep low over the rivers in a steep turn to spot salmon. You can see their red bodies from several hundred feet in the air! Whether or not you are after salmon or rainbows, if you find one, you will find the other. The rainbows are never far behind the salmon, picking up the loose eggs and any flesh coming off of the salmon bodies.

Accompanying you to the river are guides whom I can say are actually as professional and talented as the Lodge brochure says. They all know their way around a river better than most of the guests, they can take care of lunch, and they will scout nearby rivers while you enjoy yourself.

Every night you return back to the lodge, where you have a nice Alaskan dining room waiting for you, and a billiard/game room with a BYOB bar for afterwards. The food is all local and very well prepared to suit anybody's taste. The Rainbow King Lodge is a small enough concern to prepare something special for you if you want it, and we found everyone who works there very friendly.

At the end of the day, you are sure to be very tired. To me, the nicest thing about the lodge itself was the big comfortable bed. You sink right in after a long day, and fall right to sleep. You must pull the thick curtains tight, as it will be light outside all night. It is a very exotic place to go, and the lodge augments that perfectly.

The contact details are:

(Winter address)
Rainbow King Lodge, PMB 126
333 South State Street, Suite V
Lake Oswego, OR 97034
Tel: +503 967 4415
Fax: +503 635 3079

(Summer address)
Rainbow King Lodge, P.O. Box 106
Lodge Iliamna, AK 99606
Tel: +907 571 1277
Fax: +907 571 1303
Email: rkl@rainbowking.com
Web: www.rainbowking.com

INDEX

Italic page numbers refer to illustrations

PETER AND BEVERLY PICKFORD'S PHOTOGRAPHY DETAILS:

Peter and Beverly Pickford are sponsored by Kodak, and all the images in this book were photographed using the best quality 35mm and 90mm films.

Peter and Beverly wish to extend their special thanks to John Crichton and Amal Jajodia of Kodak.

All 35mm color photographs were shot on Kodachrome Professional 64 ASA film. All large-format photographs were shot on Kodak Ektachrome 100 ASA film.

Since all their equipment had be carried on their backs in waterproof bags, up and down river banks, in boats of all kinds, in light aircraft and Jumbo jets, they limited themselves to the bare necessities.

Their equipment consisted of:

Nikon F4 camera bodies (x3)

Nikon F5 camera body

Linhof Landscape camera with 90mm lens

Nikon AF 28mm f2.8 lens

Nikon AF 80-200mm f2.8 zoom lens

Nikon AF 35-70mm f2.8 zoom lens

Nikkor AF 300mm f2.8 lens

Nikkor AF macro f2.8 lens

Nikkor 15mm Ultra Wide f3.5 lens

Nikkor TC 300 lens adaptor

Minolta Flash meter III

Nikon SB 25 Flash

Nikon SB 26 Flash

Manfrotto Tripod Model ★055

For underwater photography they used a waterproof housing and an Eikelite sub-strobe flash.

Peter and Beverly also wish to thank Land Rover, South Africa

Other books by the Pickfords include:

The Miracle Rivers - The Okavango and Chobe of Botswana by Peter and Beverly Pickford, Southern Book Publishers (Pty) Ltd, 1999.

First published in 2001 by New Holland Publishers (UK) Ltd

London   Cape Town   Sydney   Auckland

2 4 6 8 10 9 7 5 3 1

Garfield House, 86–88 Edgware Road, London W2 2EA

80 McKenzie Street, Cape Town 8001, South Africa

Level 1/Unit 4, 14 Aquatic Drive, Frenchs Forest, NSW 2086, Australia

218 Lake Road, Northcote, Auckland, New Zealand

ISBN 1 85974 937 2

Edited and designed by
Design Revolution Limited, Brighton
Project Editor: Ian Whitelaw
Designer: Lucie Penn
Editor: Julie Whitaker

Index by Indexing Specialists, Hove

Production: Joan Woodroffe
Publishing Director: Yvonne McFarlane

Reproduction by Colourscan (Singapore)
Printed and bound in Singapore by Kyodo Printing Co (Singapore) Pte Ltd